All my best!

Lessons from the Road

INSPIRATIONAL
INSIGHTS

BY LEADING SPEAKERS IN EDUCATION

Zing!

Leadership
Development Systems, LLC

Just add people.

Published by Zing! Leadership Development Systems, LLC
Box 1041
Marion, MA 02738
www.zingleadership.com
1.888.566.7536

Zing! Leadership Development Systems, LLC

Lessons from the Road: Inspirational Insights by Leading Speakers in Education
Includes bibliographical references.
ISBN-10: 0-9792134-0-1
ISBN-13: 978-0-9792134-0-3

Printed in the United States of America
FIRST EDITION
10 9 8 7 6 5 4 3 2 1

Cover Design and Layout by Josh Visser
Printed by Color House Graphics, Grand Rapids, Michigan

Dedication

To those who make the world a better place through the giving of their time, talent, knowledge, personality, faith, sense of humor, compassion, leadership, diligence, love, kindness, concern, activism, commitment, creativity—to name a few gifts; the most special of which is presence.

Acknowledgements

The sincerest of appreciation is extended to all who played a role in the formation and production of this book, including the initial readers and editors: Anthony Butler (lead editor), Joe Carver, Diana Macfarlane, George Ranville, and Johnnie Tuitel. Gratitude is also extended to Ami Milano, Ami Hughes, Josh Visser, Chris Hughes, Jermaine M. Davis, Rick Barnes, Joel Goldman and Kaitlin Denney for their expertise, assistance and support. From what began as a simple concept and grew into a way to serve others through the additional charitable efforts of the authors, it is a blessing to work so collaboratively with colleagues and friends sincerely dedicated to making a difference in the world.

Table of Contents

EFFECTIVE COMMUNICATION

FAMILY

LIFE

LOVE AND COMPASSION

RELATIONSHIPS

SUCCESS

THINKING DIFFERENTLY

WISDOM AND REFLECTION

Foreword

From winning Olympic Gold to beating cancer, I've learned the value of doing what it takes to get the job done—to achieve success. In short, there is no substitute for hard work, commitment and faith. Success is a personal concept, however, and can only be defined by the individual who will—or will not—put forth the effort to achieve their goal; whether this is to excel at a particular sport, be the best parent possible, or rebuild your life after surviving a natural disaster. Therefore, as you grow and change, so does your definition of success.

Being on the road as a skater for so many years has taught me many lessons about life, people and what it means to successful. For example, the road has taught me each audience is a new audience with high expectations and a desire to be entertained, thrilled and excited by those of us willing to put ourselves out there night after night, year after year, and decade after decade. The road has taught me that true success involves the unselfish use of your talents to bring others joy, help others achieve and serve humanity. It is the process of raising others up through your good intention and making the world better than you found it. Finally, the road has shared with me some of life's tougher lessons like; life isn't always fair, it takes great faith to keep going when you are tired or dealt a bad hand, and knowing whose advice or guidance to trust.

Over the past four decades, many people have given me advice or tried to teach me something I didn't know. It wasn't always easy to know whose opinion or advice to follow with immediate changes in my behavior and attitude, and whose remarks—albeit well intentioned were not going to serve me well. Is it possible to trust the advice without trusting its source? Or, is the very act of good intention enough? Now that my time on the road also includes speaking on motivation and success, I am more aware than ever of the importance of these two questions because in order to motivate someone into action, they must have some degree of trust in you. Whether gained through one's professional career, knowledge, training, accomplishments, character or life experience, it is important to consider how trust is born. I believe the scales of truth are tipped in the direction of listening to those who practice what they teach, continuously seek a higher ground, and live, lead and love through their faith.

Lessons from the Road: Inspirational Insights by Leading Speakers in Education is a collection of inspirational insights by thirty-eight individuals dedicated to teaching others how to achieve their goals in secondary and higher education, as well as, in non-profit helping organizations. The authors represent a diverse group of professional speakers, student affairs practitioners, university presidents and educators committed to serving the greater social good. Their words of advice, thoughts on success and inspirational insights are offered to you as an instructional life guide—if you are ready to learn.

My parents were both college professors. I always admired their different styles of teaching and approaches to inspiring learning. My father didn't want anyone in his class to come "just to earn a grade." They had to learn something. He rewarded effort but gave very few "A's." My mother, on the other hand, had a style that was based on nurturing students to get in touch with what made them unique. They could apply her lessons in a more personal and long lasting manner.

I invite you to consider how the pages to follow can be a lasting positive influence on your life. What can you learn? Go ahead and trust the sources of inspiration—with a few exceptions, their classroom is on the road and their words are as diverse as their experiences. Allow the words of those with not only good intentions, but good advice learned in a variety of ways—including their life on the road, to help you move forward in your relationships, community involvement, education, faith and life. Let them inspire you to achieve success—however you define it.

Scott Hamilton

Introduction

Kierkegaard once said, "Death is ultimate teacher." He meant that death is our common destiny, and as such, it should teach us not to waste time or squander our precious lives on unworthy events or causes. I have used this teaching to stay active, involved, and focused on the precious gift that is life. With all its trials and tribulations, life is a gift, a blessing, an amazing time span in which we have an unlimited number of experiences to live out in a very finite amount of time.

The road is another great and ultimate teacher. On the road— away from the familiar, facing the unexpected and unplanned for—the traveler is faced with him or her self; face to face. The road is a university with colleges in geography, art, anthropology, sociology, communication, heath and physical education, math and science, environment, human relations, architecture, business, and travel and leisure, to name but a few. Over the next rise is the next miracle. Is it a cloud formation or an amazing city? Is it a convenience store clerk with a great attitude or the best food you never ate before? A language you have never heard or an animal you have never seen in the wild?

We are blessed to have gathered in this book a group of individuals (also known as "road warriors") who have traveled in every State in the Union, most Provinces in Canada, several nations around the world, and down every major, and most minor, highways and back roads you have ever heard and not heard of. The road has taught them powerful lessons they willingly share with you, the reader.

When Peter Carr asked his uncle, Thomas Jefferson, his advice on traveling, Mr. Jefferson said, "Stay home." When you travel your attention and affections are spread over an increasingly wide array of people and places. When you are gone, you will long for home. When you are home, you will wonder what is happening in the places you have returned home from. Thought provoking, to say the least!

Father Henri Nouwen wrote in one of his delightful books that Jesus sent the Disciples out in pairs to keep them honest. I have traveled with my children enough to know he was right. Everything I said on the road found its way back to my wife Donna's ears and it was just simply easier to tell the truth! You can rest assure the "road warriors" and contributors to this book are telling you at least their version of the truth!

I believe you will enjoy the many inspirational insights and lessons to follow. So sit back, open *Lessons from the Road: Inspirational Insights by Leading Speakers in Education*, and have a good read on us.

Dr. Will Keim

Difference Makers

BOTHER TO BE A
ROLE MODEL

"Above all, we must realize that each of
us makes a difference with our life.
Each of us impacts the world around us every single day.
We have a choice to use the gift of life to make
the world a better place—or, not to bother."

- Jane Goodall

Jane Goodall is famous through out the world for working with chimpanzees. Her respect, dedication and affection for animals is incredible. Her life is a testimony to the effect of passionate living and the potential impact one's life can have on others, even an entire culture. Her life story is one of adventure, courage, and the unknown. Jane Goodall role modeled the value of being true to yourself by blazing new ways of thinking about human nature through her work with chimpanzees. She created her life's path, as she lived it.

Ever wonder what path or direction you were destined to follow? Ever struggle with feeling different or alone? Do you sometimes feel you're out of place, as if you don't really fit in? Do you feel like the rest of the world is tuned to Channel 3 and you're hearing Channel 4? You don't know what it is, but you feel out of balance, uncomfortable, dissatisfied, and lost. You want so badly to feel internal peace, yet there is something missing.

You are not alone. Many people share this loss of direction, and feeling of sadness and dissatisfaction. But you can choose to make them fleeting moments, a temporary detour in your life's journey, or accept them as "just the way it was meant to be." I say: Take action! Do something to fix what's broken! Get found if you are lost!

The source of your unhappiness, or feelings of confusion, may in fact come from "the GAP." Not the store, but the gap in your life. Is there consistency between your actions, "the doing," and your belief system, "the knowing?" When "the doing" and "the knowing" don't match, the outcome is dissatisfaction.

Investing time and effort to close the gap is how you make a difference, and provide a role model to the world that you are confident in your choices. When you continue to push forward, work on your personal development, and improve your skills, the gap is replaced with potential. Every time you try something new, you grow and discover your own truth.

Nelson Mandela said, "Our deepest fear is not that we are inadequate. It is that we are powerful beyond measure." The more you try new things and discover your own potential, the fuller your life will become, and the more you will know what brings you joy. How or where do you start to find this truth? Three ways: Focus on your good stuff, understand yourself and your space, and take action.

Focus on Your Good Stuff. The strongest places to operate are from your strengths and (or) where you are most competent. Your competence leads to your confidence. And when you feel confident you are more likely to be successful.

One of the best lessons in life I ever learned came when I received a term paper heavily marked with red ink. There was barely any white left on the page! I interpreted the red ink as everything I had done wrong. I could barely breathe. Seeing my distress, the professor approached me and explained, "Patty, you know what you don't do well; I wanted to draw attention to what you do well."

Do you spend valuable time looking at what others are doing and trying to measure up to their skills? Do you focus on what you don't do well? Look hard at your skills and abilities. Take pride in what you enjoy doing, and in those parts of you that make you feel totally alive and vibrant!

When you focus on your good stuff, you operate from the space of your competence which leads to increased confidence. To start the journey of discovering your truth, consider what you really enjoy doing, or excel at doing. Can you feel the gap closing? Are you beginning to role model consistency between what you want and what you do?

Understand Yourself and Your Space. You are with yourself all the time. I'll prove it to you. Take a pen and draw two circles at least an inch wide. In one of the circles draw the front side of a penny and draw the back side of a penny in the other circle. The Jeopardy theme song is playing in the background...

Now, look at a penny. How many parts or elements did you correctly draw? Did you remember the word "Liberty" on the front? Which way is Abe Lincoln's head facing? Did you remember the phrase "E Pluribus Unum?"—meaning "out of the many, one" which appears on the back side? Whether you actually drew the circles or just tried to picture it in your mind, I bet you weren't able to recall all of the elements.

The US Mint says that we touch about 1,000 pennies every year. Why couldn't you remember what a penny looks like? Just because you are familiar with something doesn't mean you are knowledgeable about it. Just because you are with yourself all the time doesn't necessarily mean you know yourself. Invest the time to explore yourself. Try doing new things. Hang out with new people. Read a book from a different genre. Learn a new language. See what you like by expanding your choices!

Another way to understand yourself is to plan a total diversion, or detour, from whatever is happening in your life. Clean your room (which can be very therapeutic for some); take a last minute trip—or, visit somewhere local, where no one can find you; spend an afternoon curled up with a book; or engage in a day of rigorous physical activity. Break from your routine and see where the day takes you!

Take Action—Build Momentum. You serve as a role model as you discover your own truth. Oprah Winfrey said, "My philosophy is that not only are you responsible for your life, but doing the best at this moment puts you in the best place for the next moment." Focus on doing what you do well today. It is through action that you put yourself in the best place to serve as a role model. Talk is easy. Here are some ways to build momentum:

- Commit to listening to music you enjoy every day.

- Commit to regularly sharing time with a friend whose very name puts a smile on your face.

- Commit to regularly playing an instrument that has always brought you pleasure.

- Commit some time every day to skateboarding if it thrills you.

- Commit to regularly working out if you love the way it energizes you for the day.

- Commit to writing in your journal daily as an expression of self-reflection and knowledge.

- Commit to making a stranger smile today, tomorrow and every day.

- Commit to looking for inspirational material every day so your brain can smile, too.

- Commit to sending a thank you card to a former teacher who taught you well.

- Commit to saying "good job" the next time someone makes you a cup of coffee or serves you.

- Commit to noticing those around you often not noticed and make their day with a "hello."

Patty Hendrickson

HARD WIRED

Genetics rock.

Have you noticed there are some unique ways we are "hard wired" to our relatives? Personality traits, work ethic, stance, eyebrows, and vocal tones, for example? Genetics are powerful, creeping up on you when you least expect it! Genetics are even more powerful when combined with similar upbringings, nurturing and family traditions.

While I've learned much from mentors and supervisors, the people who taught me the most were my relatives, and their complex cocktail of chromosomes is my driving force. My great grandmother, Angelina, was an immigrant from Italy. On settling in New York City, she became very involved in the ratification of the 19th Amendment, giving women the right to vote. No woman descended from her has been able to be controlled by men. I am a proud of this lineage.

Great Grandma Angelina bore two children, Lydia and Flavia. Lydia, my great aunt, married an olive oil tycoon, and upon returning from their honeymoon, she had her marriage annulled. She became a flapper and drank and danced her way through the roaring 20's. She never re-married.

Advice from my great aunt Lydia usually turned to issues around women's liberation and sex. Although I never paid much attention to some of her advice on sex (she was, from my youthful point of view, old, and getting her advice on the topic was creepy,) I did appreciate the liberating spirit in which it was intended.

Flavia was my maternal grandmother. She became an art teacher and married a high school math teacher named Edward. Grandma Flavia became the department head for all art education in the Merrick, Long Island School District, and Grandpa Eddie became a principal. From their tradition, educators have sprung forth in my family. My mother is a teacher, my uncle a college professor and coach. I work in higher education as a university administrator.

Grandma Flavia's approach to education was one of encouragement, quality and inclusion. She believed art class was a place where those disenchanted with other course work could find their muse. She embraced every student with care and provided them with the best art supplies taxpayers' money could buy.

I am hard wired the same way. If you were to go into my office, for example, you'd see an $80 set of Prisma Color magic markers. These are my markers and only I use them. I have some cheap Crayola markers for general use, but the Prisma Colors are mine. (Although my grandmother strongly believed in student inclusion, she also liked to have a set of items for her own use.)

Grandpa Eddie's approach to education was feared by some and admired by many! When it came to disciplining students, let's just say if he implemented today what he employed back then, he'd most likely be saddled with a few lawsuits. Oh, he never hit a student. His technique was more creative.

Disruptive and ill-mannered students would often find their way to the "sand room." This was a brightly lit room located in the basement of the school with a two-inch layer of sand from one wall to the other. The room was used for messy, large scale art projects. When a student was brought to the "sand room," Grandpa Eddie would draw a circle around their feet. As he raked himself out of the room (much like a sand trap at a golf course,) he would make sure the student was clear on why they were there. By raking himself out of the room, the student was trapped—and forced to reflect upon his or her actions and the consequences.

Back then, parents supported this method of discipline. It got results. In fact, one trip to the "sand room" did the trick. My grandfather's recidivism rate was impressive. His intent was never to embarrass or demean a student; rather, he strove to teach them.

When Grandpa Eddie passed away from colon cancer, bag after bag of letters and cards from past students and parents arrived at Grandma Flavia's door. The majority of these condolences credited my grandfather as having been a major force in their growth and eventual success in life.

I am hard wired the same way. As an educator, I too seek to impose sanctions derived from considerable thought and purpose. I also believe students must understand the impact their actions make on the community at large. Additionally, I do it with an appropriate degree of humor and frankness.

My grandparents taught me another invaluable lesson: Not everyone gets a trophy. In this day and age of "instant gratification" it's a hard, but valuable, principle to grasp.

Only those who truly deserved awards received them from my grandparents. They were model educators, encouraging those who weren't achieving well in one area to try something for which they were better suited. I can hear them saying, "Well, let's find something you are good at, and let's get cracking!"

I am hard wired. When a student wants recognition for meeting their basic academic requirements, I explain to them that equals the passing grade of a "C." There isn't anything wrong with a well-earned "gentleman's C." It just doesn't come with the same bells and whistles as an "A."

The idea of a well-earned "C" is difficult for many students to grasp on today's campus. Students clearly seek the "effort" grade, or the self-perceived grade, not the actual earned grade as defined by the instructor or professor. I remember my grandparents and use more modern language to say, "Let's get cracking!"

When my grandparents retired from education, they left their schools in a state where their successors could take the reigns and move on. They demonstrated that despite their success and influence, they too were replaceable. Younger professionals assumed their positions, new practices became commonplace, and things continued to change for the better.

I am hard wired. I know that I am replaceable, and the best I can do is my best. I understand the power found in respecting higher education, our institutional mission, the students and community we serve. I understand the importance of leaving a place better than you found it—leaving it ready for the next educator to make an impression.

With such great wiring, why would I ever question myself? How do I know when to do what comes naturally, or when it's time to think for myself?

I've always sought the approval of my grandparents, Flavia and Eddie. That's probably because both individually, and as a pair, they looked like someone I wanted to become. They were difference-makers. They were incredible people who composed my personal root system and connected me to the soil. Do you have a relative who does the same for you? Are you hard wired?

I am hard wired. Therefore, I must continue growing towards a more enlightened future. While learning from my heritage, I remain committed to a certain degree of personal curiosity, which fuels my enthusiasm and creativity. My personal space is dedicated to growth, learning and positive energy. No matter how old I get, I believe I will always stop and wonder, "Would I be making grandma and grandpa proud of me right now? Let's see, at this moment, would I be a "C" or "A" in their eyes?"

Laura De Veau

INSPIRED LEADERSHIP

Do you know someone who fits the description of an "inspired leader?"

What do they say and do on a daily basis? What enables them to motivate others? Here's a rather difficult look in the mirror: Do they respond differently to most situations than you would? Think back on your experiences. Think about an inspired leader who touched your life. Sometimes you have to look all the way back to your youth.

My first experience with a real leader took place when I was twelve. I used to walk to a nearby shopping mall and play video games, people-watch, and hang out with my friends. One Saturday afternoon, I saw two mimes performing in the mall. They were doing a mechanical robot routine. I was mesmerized.

At home that evening, I practiced the mechanical robot impression over and over again until I had it right. The next day, I hurried back to the mall hoping to watch the mimes perform again. For the next five weeks, I followed the mimes, Tommy and Katie. Everywhere they went, I went.

One day I worked up the courage to speak to one of the mimes. Between performances, I approached him and said, "I can do what you do!"

He said, "Well, let's see, little man."

I proudly did my mechanical routine. His response was a simple, "Come back tomorrow."

That night I could hardly sleep, thinking about the next day. I woke up and dressed quickly. I was one of the first people at the mall. This day was different, though. Tommy had gathered some of the mall executives, along with the entertainment director, before I arrived.

"Show them what you showed me yesterday," he said.

I did my robot routine. When I finished, they looked at Tommy and said, "So?"

"I want you to hire this kid for the summer," Tommy replied. "I'll teach and mentor him."

With a laugh, they replied, "Tommy, you're one of the best mimes in all of Los Angeles. Why would we hire some kid off the street?"

"Why?" repeated Tommy. "Because if you don't, I quit."

"We have no budget," a mall executive countered, "Be reasonable, Tommy."

"You'll pay him five dollars an hour. You can take it out of my pay." Tommy ended the conversation, and my life as a mime began. How can a mime, of all people, be an inspired leader?

Tommy understood the difference he could make in the life of a kid fascinated with his craft. I grew to understand Tommy's passion, dedication and burning desire to succeed. As I worked with Tommy to hone my skill, I also grew into a rather successful professional mime!

I had performed professionally for fifteen years: mime, juggler, fire eater, and magician. I used to juggle three balls to the tune of "Dueling Banjos." I tried to juggle five balls at once, but failed miserably each time.

Some time later, a friend invited me to my first juggling convention. I was never much into clubs or associations. The convention was about what I expected: a large room filled with people juggling balls, knives, and bowling balls, while passing pins, unicycling, etc.

While I watched the jugglers, a young boy no older than fourteen caught my eye. He was standing about three feet away. Why hadn't I noticed him sooner? He was a pretty typical-looking kid: jeans, T-shirt hanging out, and tennis shoes. He had a beautiful blue velvet bag.

I watched him reach into his velvet bag and pull out five shiny new juggling balls. I thought to myself, "In your dreams, kid."

Amazingly, this young boy juggled five balls for what seemed like an eternity, never dropping one. When he stopped, all five balls had fallen back into his bag—and he walked away as if it were nothing spectacular! What? I had been juggling for fifteen years and he was only fourteen years old. I was dumbfounded.

That moment, I had two choices. One, I could kill him. Two, I could reevaluate my self-imposed limitations and my fear of failing. Needless to say, no one died that day. However, two days later, at four o'clock in the morning, my wife woke up to me in the other room screaming, "I did it, I did it! I can juggle five balls!"

We can all be inspired leaders. Whether you are an expert in your field like Tommy was, or a relative newcomer, like the young juggler I met, you have the opportunity to inspire greatness in others.

Maybe you won't know what it's like to juggle five balls at the same time. Maybe you won't become a professional mime. But you can and will find the best success in the things that drive you—the things you are most passionate about.

And, as you inspire others, you'll realize the reward for inspired leadership is watching someone reach their true potential, knowing you helped them along the way.

Curtis Zimmerman

MRS. NIXON

"Injustice anywhere is a threat to justice everywhere."

- Dr. Martin Luther King, Jr.

Mrs. Nixon was my seventh grade English teacher and I hated her. Yup. I hated the woman. I think I hated her because she made us work. Every Friday we were supposed to come to class prepared to do an oral book report. Of course I did what any smart seventh grader would do. I thought of all the books I'd read up to that point and lined them up. Unfortunately, I ran out of books after four Fridays.

One morning, Mrs. Nixon announced that we were only to read biographies that week and we should be prepared to report on our book on Friday. I thought, "Great, narrow down our choices, won't you?" Off to the library I went. My first task was to choose a book. I used a very scientific method—turning the book on its side and seeing how many pictures were in the center. Bingo! Lots of pictures meant a great book! Turning the book over, I noticed that it was a biography of Dr. Martin Luther King, Jr. "Perfect!" I thought. Because I knew the story, I could focus on what I loved most—the presentation.

Let me explain. I was known for my creative presentations in the seventh grade. I knew in order to get an "A+," I had to do more. My previous Friday presentations consisted of posters, show and tell, graphs and pictures. The class must have thought, "Thank you, Vernon. There goes the curve!" My presentations were becoming legendary so I began to think about what to do on this particular Friday. Flipping through the card catalogue, I ran across a slide presentation on Dr. King's life. Excellent. I borrowed the rickety audio-visual cart with the slide projector on it and rolled it into class that Friday. To the glaring looks of my peers, I set up my cart, sat down and waited for Mrs. Nixon to call on me.

Finally, Mrs. Nixon said, "Vernon, you're next." I made my way to the front of the class and delivered my introductory comments on Dr. Martin Luther King, Jr. After my opening remarks, I pressed play on the slide projector and the "I have a Dream" speech began, accompanied by my vivid slides. As the slide show played, my classmates did what 7th graders typically do: played with their gum and wrote notes back and forth, "I like you. Do you like me? Check One: Yes, No, Maybe."

As the slide show continued, I felt something happening. An odd feeling gathered in my gut and traveled up to my throat. Everyone knows that an "A+" presentation consists of opening comments, a slide show and closing comments. I knew, however, that at the end of the slide show, I was not going to be able to speak. This lump was lodged in my throat.

I noticed that Mrs. Nixon had her famous "teacher face" on. It's the face that says, "I see that something is happening to you and I know what it is!" I thought to myself, "I really hate her."

The slideshow ended. What seemed like 20 minutes was really only 20 seconds. I stood there unable to speak. How could I? I felt my classmate's eyes on me. I heard nothing. The silence was deafening. Mrs. Nixon got up from her desk and walked toward me. She put her hand on my shoulder and said: "Vernon, this is the first time you've actually heard this speech isn't it?"

This woman is crazy! How many times had I seen the "I Have a Dream" speech on television? It's framed in our living room and I've recited it at church. Why is she asking me if I've actually ever heard the speech? What is she talking about? Miraculously, I spoke. "No, Mrs. Nixon," I said. "I read the book." Mrs. Nixon replied, "That is not what I said. What I said was: This is the first time you've actually HEARD this speech isn't it?" The showman was speechless.

Mrs. Nixon was right. At that moment, I believe my ability to connect the head to the heart began—and it was all because of Mrs. Nixon. Even as a seventh grader I could make the connection between how I think and how I feel.

Many years later, I have built upon the connection between head and heart. It's so easy to say things like: "Discrimination is wrong," "People should be treated equally," and "We are the world, we are the children," but if you still let others around you become marginalized, victimized and treated unfairly without doing any-thing about it, what are your actions really saying? How can you live freely when others are held to unwritten rules and practices? What are you doing to right the wrongs in your immediate envi-ronment, community and place of employment?

To be honest, I love Mrs. Nixon. I love her for introducing me to my life's dream—a world of inclusion and social justice. The dream involves every citizen. The dream becomes more real to you when you reflect on a time when you were treated as "less than." The dream becomes more real to you when you see others treated as "less than." Let me ask directly: Have you connected your head to your heart?

Thank you, Mrs. Nixon, for such a valuable life lesson.

Vernon A. Wall

REFLECTIONS

When you look in the mirror, who do you see?
  A person who knew just what to be,
  a giver of their heart, soul and mind,
  the reflection of an educator, is that what you find?

When you look in the mirror, what looks back?
  A pair of eyes seeing beyond white or black,
  a set of shoulders strong enough for play,
  the face of compassion, is that what you'd say?

When you look in the mirror, what do you hear?
  The sounds of laughter, giggles and cheer,
  a sense of perspective, someone quietly standing tall,
  lighthearted echoes, is that what's bouncing off your wall?

When you look in the mirror, are you able to unwind?
  Go ahead and smile back at the gifted one so kind,
  because you—unlike others—have known from the start,
  ordinary clay can be molded into priceless art.

When you look in the mirror, congratulate the person you see!
  For there is a person who knew just what to be,
  creating the future in a variety of ways,
  one child at a time, is that how it plays?

When you look in the mirror, study the glass!
    For your true value isn't found in just one pass,
    and when the reflection seems foggy, even hard to reach,
    never forget, it takes a special spirit to teach!

Nancy Hunter Denney

THE VALUE OF
STALKING A MENTOR

Not too long ago, I met a young man who had heard me speak six years ago. I am frequently amazed by what a person takes from my remarks. This individual shared not only what he recalled, but how he had applied it to his life. My advice was simply: Find someone you want to be like and "stalk" them.

Stalking is against the law so my instruction was one with educational intent. My point is straightforward: When you meet someone you admire, and find that person engaged in a profession or activity that interests you, do as much as you can to spend time with that person. I learned this lesson as a college student.

I arrived at Auburn University in the fall of 1988 with a big perm and what I thought was the hippest wardrobe. Coming from a small town, I was a bit out of place and a bit out of my league. When I was asked to select a major, I recalled that women in my small town ended up following one of two professions: teaching or nursing. The latter was out of the question. I had never been very good at science or biology. So, by default, I ended up majoring in education.

I never wanted to be a teacher. At the age of 18 though this was the only option I thought was available. How silly it seems now—to even ask someone that age to declare anything, let alone a major!

Soon I discovered that there were other options available to me, but I didn't discover them in the classroom. My sorority experience opened many doors. It introduced me to wonderful people who became sources of inspiration. College ended up being what it was always intended to be—a transforming experience!

My senior year, I was introduced to Debbie Shaw, a woman I would soon "stalk." She advised the sororities on campus, and I had just been elected chapter president. I observed her calmness and immediately knew I wanted to emulate her many positive traits.

In the spring of my senior year, I called my unsuspecting mentor to arrange a meeting. I began by saying, "Tell me how you got here, and work backwards, please." She shared her story as I took notes. I used that "road map" to set my own plans. This helped me direct the course of my life. Throughout the years, I've stayed in touch with Debbie and continue to ask for guidance and support, knowing she will always be there for me.

Do you have a mentor? Who is your career role model? Is there someone you admire, and desire to be like? My version of "stalking" requires you—the "stalkee"—to make the first move. Here are five simple tips:

1. Find someone involved in an activity or profession which interests you.

2. Express your admiration in person.

3. Set up a meeting with the goal of learning how he or she arrived at that place.

4. Continue to observe and interact with this person.

5. Express your appreciation. It is your job to stay in touch with your mentor—not the other way around.

How do you find something you enjoy doing and get paid to do? Sometimes, you just need to find someone you admire and observe him or her! This is a simple concept with powerful results. Of course, you can also visit career centers, guidance counselors, or stick with a major (or career path) that doesn't bring you happiness.

It's your job to find a path that will bring you a sense of value and contribution. Start looking around...it's time to "stalk" those you admire and want to model your life after!

Dr. Lori Hart Ebert

Determination

ADVENTURES
IN HANDICAPITALISM

"When you take the focus off of yourself and put it on what
truly matters, it will change your life forever."

Each morning, Mom would take me out the back door to a set of parallel bars that were cemented into the driveway. There, she'd help me with my physical therapy. Removing an old wicker rug beater from a nail on the corner of the garage, she'd clip my heels to teach me how to walk heel to toe. "Move it!" she'd shout. "Come on, move it! We're going to make a miracle happen!"

One day, after my usual workout with Mom, she removed my leg braces and put me in a bathtub full of warm water. My legs and arms felt tight and tired, but the water was soothing.

Mom looked at me and said, "Johnnie do you know how sick you were after you were born? Do you know how sick I was after you were born? Do you know we both almost died?"

"Yeah, Mom," I answered. "You've told me that before."

But she continued. "When you were eighteen months old, the doctor told us you would never walk. He said you'd never talk, and that you'd be dependent on your family for the rest of your life. He told us to put you in an institution and let the state take care of you so we could go and have 'normal' children."

I'd heard all this before so asked her what her point was. She swiped some strands of hair out of my eyes and smiled. "Johnnie, I wish that doctor was alive today so he could see your face. You're cute. You're smart. And if you work hard and make the right choices, I believe you can change the world."

That conversation took place over thirty years ago. Now I look back on my life and realize my mom was right. My life hasn't always been easy. In fact, parts of it I wouldn't wish on anyone. But the fact of the matter is, when you take the focus off yourself and put it on what truly matters, you can change the world.

Background. Shortly after my mother's appendix ruptured, I came into this world three and a half months premature and weighing only one pound, four ounces. My infant body was placed into an incubator, and I was given oxygen to help me breathe. Unknown at the time, I received too much oxygen, which caused permanent brain damage. My parents and family soon discovered I'd been given the gift of cerebral palsy.

As a result of my cerebral palsy (it affects people in different ways and to different degrees), I've spent the majority of my life in a wheelchair. Regardless, today I am many things and lead a blessed life as an internationally recognized children's book author, philanthropist, husband, and father of three—to name a few of my "titles." I also like to call myself America's Pioneer Handicapitalist!^{SM}

Why America's Pioneer Handicapitalist? I've been a pioneer, in one way or another, my whole life. Being the third of five children born to immigrant Dutch parents, and the first born in America, by default I became the first American Tuitel.

After attending a special school for kids with disabilities for the first few years of my elementary education, I finally had a chance to attend a regular school with my brothers and sisters. In fact, I was the first student legally mainstreamed in the state of Michigan, under public law PL94-142. I'd taken another pioneering step that helped set the benchmarks for including students with disabilities into the normal classroom.

In 1999, I was first quoted by the Wall Street Journal for using the term *handicapitalism*. I used it in the context that despite my disability I was a valuable member of society who had money to spend and the right to spend it.

Since that time, it has evolved into much more than that. Now *handicapitalism* means I have just as many rights to participate in our society as everyone else. It means I have the ability to make money like everyone else and, more importantly to me, it means I have the ability to give back to the country I love.

Basically, the catchword *handicapitalism* encompasses the deliberate steps I take to develop my abilities and opportunities by cultivating good habits and working steadily to create a successful life. It's about capitalizing on a situation by surrounding myself with capable people—asking for help when help is needed. And it is about not letting my disability hold me back.

Getting Off the System—How Handicapitalism Changed My Life. It all started in 1987 when I was a junior at Hope College, a small private Christian college in Holland, Michigan. Because I used a wheelchair and was clinically diagnosed with cerebral palsy, I qualified for disability compensation from the government. This meant that each month $800 was deposited into my savings account, and it had to be spent. If more than $1,000 was accumulated, the government could take away my disability pay.

At the time I thought I was living a dream. Tuition, books, and my room and board were paid for. Money showed up each month for me to spend at my discretion. So I did what any other college kid would do. I spent the majority of my time going to concerts, attending parties, and making road trips with my fraternity brothers. I had yet to come to terms with my disability, so I acted irresponsibly as a way to deal with the pain and anger I faced because of it. I honestly felt society owed me the money because people had no idea about the difficulties I faced each day, as I tried coping with the fact that I was never going to walk.

Shortly before I left for a significant stomach operation, I had a conversation with a college professor that reinforced the idea that society owed me something. I had stopped by his office to notify him of my leave and his response shocked me then, and still remains fresh in my memory. He said, "Johnnie, don't come back to class. You don't need to come back. You're disabled, you're in a wheelchair, and the government will give you the money you need so you will never have to work a day in your life." I disagreed with his comments because I felt an education was what would make me equal in an able-bodied world.

I went back to college, finished my degree and got a job as a schoolteacher. After three years of teaching I became aware of a procedure called a dorsal rhizotomy where doctors would sever nerves in the spinal cord to help correct the spasticity often associated with cerebral palsy. Some time later, after a lot of interviews with doctors, I was scheduled to go under the knife and have the operation as a way to help me lead a slightly more normal life.

I continued on with the procedure and eventually started working with therapists who helped enable my stiff muscles to move again. They also taught me how to do everyday tasks like eating and dressing myself. I even had to take a class on tumbling where they taught me the proper way to fall.

My doctors and physical therapists evaluated me and wrote a prescription for a new wheelchair that would accommodate the physical changes resulting from the surgery. I submitted the prescription to my insurance company.

As I sat in my hospital room recovering from the day's rehab, the nurse brought my mail, which included a letter from my insurance company. They were denying coverage for a new wheelchair—a new set of "legs" to help me get from point A to point B.

My dad came in the room and could tell I was upset. "What's wrong, Johnnie?" he asked.

"The insurance company isn't going to buy me a new wheelchair. This is wrong!" I screamed.

"Calm down, Johnnie. I'll buy your chair. Your mother and I have the money and we love you. We'll get it for you."

But the emotions in me still raged. "They aren't going to cover it because they don't think I need it. What about my roommate who needs a new chair too? What if they don't think he needs one?"

My dad couldn't understand my dilemma. He said, "Well he's not my son. I'm not going to buy him one, but I'll buy you one."

"That's the point, Dad. If this is happening to me then it's happening to my roommate; it's happening to the guy down the hall, and it could be happening to anyone else in a wheelchair as well."

At that moment I came to terms with my disability, finally realizing that I was never going to walk. It was time to stop thinking about just myself, get off the system and start helping other people become successful.

Handicapitalism in Action—Taking a Risk. When I finally owned up to the fact I had a disability and could still make a difference in the world, I told my dad I wanted to talk. Together we started discussing my desire to quit my job as a schoolteacher and start my own business. My goal was to create a foundation that would purchase wheelchairs for people who couldn't afford them; I also wanted to share my story to offer hope and inspiration to others. My father thought I was crazy but agreed to loan me the money to get started.

A short time later I met George Ranville, a local businessman who was trying to get a wheelchair for his brother-in-law. He had gone through an experience similar to mine. We realized that we had to start this organization to ensure people wouldn't be prevented from participating in our free society because of mobility needs. Everyone should have the basic means to get around.

In 1995, we officially started Alternatives in Motion, a nonprofit 501(c)(3) organization whose mission is to purchase wheelchairs for individuals who lack health insurance or other financial means. Our first wheelchair recipient was a woman who became paralyzed from the waist down after being stabbed by an intruder in her college apartment. That first year, she, along with fifteen other people, received new wheelchairs from Alternatives in Motion. We had the momentum we needed to make the organization even more successful.

Ten years later, our dream is still thriving. Alternatives in Motion continues to help people obtain wheelchairs. Through the support of foundations, individuals, fund-raisers, and lots of hard work, we have been able to give away over 650 wheelchairs to people in 18 states and 130 Michigan communities at an average cost of $4,000-$8,000 per chair.

Handicapitalizing on the Future. My vision was becoming a reality. In addition, I was able to get off the system and start making money for myself as a successful businessman. Throughout this journey, I learned that we all have various disabilities. It's the way we choose to overcome those disabilities that will make us successful. The only thing that is different between people like me and those who have other disabilities is mine is more visible because of the wheelchair.

Shortly after the creation of Alternatives in Motion, we created another company called Tap Shoe Productions, which focuses on reaching people of all ages through my Gun Lake Adventure Series (an internationally recognized children's book series) and educational presentations. Proceeds from these businesses are pumped back into our charity to continue helping others get the mobility equipment to which they're entitled.

Final Words of Inspiration. I'm 43 years old, and I'm never going to walk. I'll spend the rest of my life in a wheelchair never knowing the simple pleasure of throwing a football in the backyard with my three boys. I'll never get to experience the warm sand between my toes as my wife and I walk down the beach hand in hand, watching the sunset.

Fortunately, through *handicapitalism* I have realized that there is a lot more to life than what your legs can or cannot do. The important things are what your mind thinks, your heart believes, and your soul lives. These are principals that you will remember long after your life here on earth.

A time will come when I'll leave this world, and I'll be walking in heaven. I can say with confidence that as I look back at my time here on Earth, people will remember me for the things I did, rather than the things I didn't do.

I challenge each and every one of you to dream big. Think about your goals and the obstacles in your way. Overcome obstacles by focusing on your own abilities and taking advantage of the opportunities that come your way. Become a handicapitalist today.

Johnnie Tuitel

ARE YOU BRAVE?

Typically, taking risks isn't something to which I would come either enthusiastically or hesitantly. Throughout my life I was somewhere in the middle—a moderate risk taker. I still consider myself in this category. Others see me quite differently. I'm sure this is because I've done my fair share of living life in front of a microphone—a place other think is reserved for the "brave." Not me.

Bravery is a label clearly up for interpretation, especially when it is being used to describe yours truly. In fact, given my history putting out fires, there's a thin line between being "brave" and being "reckless."

In my younger professional days, I was a "residence director." A resident director oversees and guides college students living on campus. I recall that one evening I was dressed only in pajamas, sans the protection of a good bra, putting out a burning trash can by picking it up with my bare hands and throwing it into a shower stall. I concluded my act of heroism by turning on the shower. Brave of me? The fire chief said I was being "reckless." We agreed to disagree.

As a more worldly and experienced professional (yet still holding onto the trash can in the shower definition of bravery) I have greater personal insight. Am I brave? Let's see...

Life at the microphone is where I feel the most at ease. It's where I find my purpose. Somewhere in the heat of the spotlights, my purpose is clear: entertain, inform, preach, excite, and inspire.

Dollars to donuts, I'd rather be in front of a crowd of 1,001. It's a great place to hide and much safer than being exposed in one on one exchanges. It's where I can make people laugh, bring them joy and share inspiring messages.

Am I brave? Does being the "opening act" or first in a lineup of speakers qualify me for this honor? Most folks hate this spot in the lineup, but I see it as an opportunity to jump on the proverbial grenade. My philosophy about life in general mirrors my life at the mic; specifically, if I really screw it up, there's time to fix it.

What most people don't realize is that being the opening act is like working with a net. Being the headliner is like being Evil Knievel jumping across the Snake River Canyon in Idaho. The "star" better stick the landing or it will be messy! I accept how far I'm willing to go.

Are you brave? Guess that all depends upon how you interpret the word.

Laura De Veau

IT'S NEVER TOO LATE

*"Waiting for others to create your destiny can take a life time.
Taking responsibility for your life creates a future worth living."*

Just when you think you're done... you're not. Life lessons are learned wherever you go and at the most inconvenient times. Some lessons are quickly taught, while others take years—if they are learned at all. Still others require you to unravel the twine of your life in a meticulous order. Then there are those lessons which have incredible power in their simplicity.

On a much welcomed flight home from St. Louis to Boston, I over heard a woman telling a gate attendant she had just graduated from college. By "just" she actually meant in 2003. Their conversation would not normally have kept my attention had I not glanced up from my computer and saw the graduate—an elderly woman who had put her cane aside and pleasantly accepted the assistance of a wheel chair to navigate the uneven jet way.

"Where did you just graduate from?" I asked looking up from my computer not minding my own business.

The very pleasant and clearly independent woman smiled warmly at me and said, "I graduated from college three years ago. My name is Sally. You know, I once overheard a classmate saying to another younger student, 'She's not like my grandmother.' I didn't know how to take that!"

I then asked, "Why? What made you go to college?"

As they began to call for passengers to board, Sally kept our conversation going as I packed up my computer and stood up, "I always enjoyed learning for learning's sake. I wanted knowledge and had the time to learn about things I didn't know—like art history and the classics." She added, "Of course I had to fulfill the core requirements like everyone else."

After exchanging pleasantries, I couldn't help myself and asked, "Sally, how old were you when you graduated?"

She didn't answer.

Instead she said with obvious pride in her accomplishment and a sincere desire to be humble, "I don't mean to brag. I tell my story only so you'll tell others. It's never too late to go to college, or get what you want in life. It's never too late to read. I satisfy my needs by doing my own thing—I read a lot of books on American history and the classic now—like Abraham Lincoln, Ben Franklin and the books like 1776."

Nothing like getting to the point, I thought. This was a woman who understood the connection between young at heart and sharp as a tack.

As luck would have it, Sally sat directly behind me on the plane. After considerable prodding, I learned more about this fascinating travel partner. I'm not sure where her story began, but I know where it ended and a few bits and pieces in between.

Sally is a loving mother of two, grandmother of five, and great grandmother of three. She was married in 1939 for what I calculated was over fifty years to a man she truly loved. After his death, she stayed active by traveling, working part time and dating. She met another special man who she has dated for the last twelve years.

"Back then, we married young," explained Sally. "I was only twenty."

I smiled thinking of my own teenage daughter being married in six years and wondered what it must have been like to be so young and unsure of yourself but in a committed relationship. Then I remembered who I was talking to...

"I started secretarial school right after I got married and got a job," Sally said sensing my thoughts.

"Not too many wives did that back then," she continued, "Guess how much I got paid a week?"

I didn't even want to venture a guess, but it was a long flight. "Let's see, how about fifty dollars?" I guessed.

"Try again," said Sally with a sense of playfulness.

"I have no idea. You tell me." I responded knowing she was enjoying our verbal game of ping pong.

"I made twelve dollars a week!" Sally continued to go into more details about her diverse work history over the past six decades which included (among other things) working in a law office, university and as an administrator for a local hospital. She didn't impress me as someone who was going to sit around.

"So, what made you go back to college?" I finally asked.

"I didn't go back. I just never went in the first place. I had always wanted to go. The time was just never right." There was a pause before Sally completed her explanation, almost as if she was considering if she would have changed anything about her past if given the chance. I got the distinct impression she was quite happy about her life.

"It was my daughter who suggested I go to college because she knew I wasn't one to sit around the house. She had the application sent to me."

As Sally explained how she got into college she seemed to get a kick out of her next comment, "They asked for my high school transcripts from 1937!"

"Did you enjoy being a college student?" I asked knowing how many times I had stood before traditionally aged students at freshmen orientation praying they knew the privilege of learning, yet accepting the reality many new students look at college today not for what they can learn, rather for what they will earn; it is sadly a means to an end—something to make it through instead of a place of intrigue, critical thinking and exploration.

"Oh, every minute of it!" answered Sally. "For me, it was so much to my advantage to be able to learn about the course work for its own sake. I felt badly for many of my classmates who were working two jobs, had families to take care of and couldn't really participate at the level I could. I was very fortunate. I could go to college to learn."

Too tired to do the math, I asked my new friend one last time about her age hoping she would prevent me from having to call her alumni office or get out a calculator, "So, how old were you when you graduated?"

Sally said with pride, "It took me seven years to graduate with a degree in General Studies. I graduated cum laude at the age of 83!"

Nancy Hunter Denney

RESPONDABILITY

Possibly the happiest day of our married life came on September 28th—five years ago. Two little pink lines confirmed it. After a year of trying, hoping and praying to become pregnant, our dream had come true. We quickly called our families and shared our exciting news. A few days later, the doctor confirmed Karin's pregnancy and a due date of May 30th, only eight months away.

The pregnancy progressed uneventfully. Aside from being tired, the mother-to-be experienced no morning sickness or high blood pressure. We were fortunate, and knew it. All we really wanted was a healthy baby—boy or girl, so had decided not to find out the gender of our baby in advance. We'd wait and be surprised.

The holiday season was filled with so many blessings to share. We went home to Minnesota to be with our families. We spent a beautiful New Year's Eve back home alone, knowing a year from now we would have a baby boy or girl to join in the celebration. It was a beautiful southern California day. The sky was cloudless and crystalline blue. The temperature was perfect as we drove up to the mountains to play in the snow and enjoy the beginning of a great new year.

Five days later, our great new year came crashing down around us. A doctor's routine office visit revealed our baby had some "anomalies indicating possible chromosomal defects." We clung to the uncertainty of his diagnosis. After two sleepless nights, we returned for an amniocentesis which would determine a variety of things, including the gender and health of our baby. It would take almost two weeks to get the results.

If you've ever had to wait to get test results, you know it is an agonizing, almost torturous process, filled with many tears, nerves and questions (most of which begin with "why") without easy answers. All you can do is cope the best way you know how. For us, that meant sharing our anxiety with those who loved us, praying, crying and learning as much as we could about our baby's possible chromosomal defects. Was it Trisomy 21 (also known as Down's Syndrome) or Trisomy 18?

The internet was a mixed blessing. How much did we really want to find out? Was it helpful to read page after page without any real medical expertise? What if the prognosis was discouraging? How was one defect "better" than the other? The information we were getting was confusing and scary, yet informative. Within the bad news, we found bits of optimism. Although these were few and far between, we clung to all hope and reminded ourselves that miracles happen every day.

Soon, we found ourselves enlisting the prayers of our family, friends and hundreds of people we didn't even know. There is great power in prayer. We also found ourselves praying for the outcome to be Down's Syndrome. That sounds odd. However, in our situation, you find yourself "picking" the lesser of two evils. At least with Down's Syndrome, our baby would have difficulties, but he or she would live. You can't hope for even that much with Trisomy 18—a very rare and fatal condition.

We learned of God's plan and were devastated. Our baby had Trisomy 18. We struggled to face the reality of our baby's condition and impending loss of a child not born. As speakers, we teach how people can't control what happens to them, only how they respond. Wow. It wasn't easy having to walk our talk. We wanted to curl up into ourselves and shut the world away. Have you ever known this feeling of complete despair and darkness? If so, you also might know that out of the darkness, light will come.

In the midst of our pain, we found strength from each other, and from our total commitment to live fully. We found solace in knowing that we would live through this tragedy, and kept pushing ahead, one day at a time. Our baby continued to grow inside of Karin. We continued to love and accept our baby boy, and appreciate him for the gift he was. We had become open to whatever path his life would take while holding tightly to our faith.

We named our unborn son, Kaleb, meaning "faithful and bold." Because of him, we were learning and growing in faith, and being bold in how we were choosing to move forward. With great optimism we registered at Babies R Us, and Karin's friends threw her a baby shower. It was a touching ceremony known as a "Blessing Way," and was filled with love, hope and prayers from the very special women in her life.

Four days later, Kaleb was born into Heaven.

In the weeks and months that followed, we held each other close. We cried together, prayed together, and mourned together. We struggled to walk our talk and there were days it was all we could do to get out of bed.

If you've experienced loss, you know the strength it takes to put one foot on the floor when all you really want to do is hide under the sheets. If you've experienced loss, you understand the relentless pain and sense of sadness. You also come to understand the choice which presents itself every day—to live your life to the fullest or to wallow in despair.

Our unborn son gave us a valuable gift. He showed us that every day you can decide to live fully, show gratitude for your many blessings, and understand the power that comes from "respondability."

When life deals you a bad hand, what will you do? Will you choose not to be destroyed? Will you choose to move forward? Will you make the decision to decide how to live your life and appreciate the many remaining gifts?

Troy and Karin Stende

RIDING THE
STRUGGLE BUS

Ever get up, put on your clothes, and get on board your only available mode of transportation—the Struggle Bus?

This is the way you get from one place to the other without any effort, without using any brain cells. If you feel like you're running uphill, backwards and naked, you've already jumped on the bus! Yes, there are days when your brain just isn't functioning.

Sometimes during my travels, I observe other people on the bus. I am not alone. In fact, I think there are permanent passengers on the Struggle Bus who have assigned seats. One such young woman took her seat just the other day...

I love Subway. You get just what you want and it's all made in front of your very eyes. No surprises. Because I love lettuce, I asked for some on my sub. Apparently, my server was concerned that her supply of lettuce was about to go bad—as many others who work there must think—because I once again received way too much lettuce.

I asked, "May I have my sub with light lettuce, please?" Much to my amusement, my server smiled at me and said, "Sir, I'm sorry but we only have one kind of lettuce."

Everyone rides the Struggle Bus at some point. I got right back on it just after the "lettuce incident." After a recent trip to the grocery store, I realized I had forgotten to pick up an item. I grudgingly went back to the store. While walking up the aisle, my cell phone rang. I got distracted with the phone call and bought additional items, but I still hadn't picked up the thing I had gone back to purchase in the first place!

Once again, as my seat on the bus stayed warm, I went back to the store and managed to buy what I needed. Walking back to my car, I was playing with my keys and dropped them. While I was on the ground trying to pick up my keys, my contact lens fell out of my eye and landed somewhere on the asphalt. People came to my rescue and before long I could see again.

Once I got home, it hit me: I left the grocery bag on the ground in the parking lot! Feeling like I was now driving the Struggle Bus, I headed back to the grocery store for the fourth time.

I guess the Struggle Bus has plenty of seats for everyone!

Judson Laipply

THE SPRING IN YOUR STEP

Beyond the autumn of our lives, and deeper than the cold of winter, lies the eternal hope of Spring within each of us.

Days to be reborn, time to blossom, to stretch, to branch out, to sing new songs, to stay up later, to breathe deeply and exercise more—or less.

Excited to feel lazy, to cut new grass, to protect the warmth of the sun on our sheltered skin, and to walk new paths that have been in hiding.

A time to clean out the cobwebs in our closets and in our minds, to pick up our yards and our pants, to dance in the puddles and swing around and flash your smile.

Anxious to guzzle more sweaty drinks with floating lemons, after tirelessly tidying up the earth and giving back to the future.

A time to be playful, to put on your Easter bonnet and don those sunglasses, and think about being a star, in your own home movie, in the theater of your mind.

So you hold your breath and into your ears creep…"And the Oscar goes to…you!" for the Spring in your step.

Patti Geib Holmes

Effective Communication

IS ANYONE LISTENING TO ME?

WHEN I ASK YOU TO LISTEN TO ME,
   and you start giving me advice,
   you have not done what I've asked;

WHEN I ASK YOU TO LISTEN TO ME,
   and you begin to tell me why I shouldn't feel this way,
   it's like you're dumping my feelings in the trash.

WHEN I ASK YOU TO LISTEN TO ME,
   and you feel like you have to solve my problem,
   you've failed me, as strange as that may seem;

LISTEN! THAT'S ALL I ASKED YOU TO DO,
   not to talk or do anything else,
   just to allow yourself to hear me.

ADVICE IS CHEAP:
   $1.25 will get you both Dear Abby and Dr. Phil
   in the same newspaper no less;

SEE, I CAN DO FOR MYSELF,
   I'm not helpless; maybe a little discouraged,
   but I'm still capable of cleaning up my own mess.

WHEN YOU DO SOMETHING FOR ME
 I can and need to do for myself,
 you contribute to my weakness and fear;

BUT, WHEN YOU ACCEPT THE SIMPLE FACT THAT I DO
 feel what I feel, no matter how irrational,
 then I can stop trying to convince you, and allow my conscience to clear.

MY "IRRATIONAL BEHAVIOR" MAY ACTUALLY MAKE SENSE
 when you fully understand
 what's behind each and every one of them;

MAYBE THAT'S WHY PRAYER WORKS SO WELL,
 because God is quiet, and He just listens,
 whenever we talk to Him.

SO PLEASE LISTEN AND JUST HEAR ME,
 and if you want to talk,
 I promise I'll listen to you;

ALL I ASK is that you wait your turn,
 and then I'll prove
 that listening is the easiest thing to do.

Dr. Joe Martin

POWERFUL WORDS

Have you ever noticed how just a few words can completely make or break a situation?

"I love you."

"Thank you."

"No thank you."

"Yes."

"No."

Simple words with huge meanings. Simple words making strong statements. Some affirmative, some not. Some in agreement, others not. It takes only a few words.

These short words have such a strong impact on us as we grow up! Some of my favorites have been shared by many. They may have been taught by a parent, grandparent, teacher or member of the clergy. But any way you think about it, these are profound statements.

"Treat others as you wish to be treated." Not some of the time. Not just when it is convenient or when it might be to your advantage. Treat others as you wish to be treated at all times. Can you imagine what the world would be like if everyone followed this statement? We would greet others with a smile or simple nod. We would open the door for others and say thank you in return. We would wave at one another as we pass on the street. And we wouldn't hold grudges, develop bad attitudes, or maintain assumptions about those we meet. It's really pretty simple—treat others as you wish to be treated.

Call home and say, "Thank you."   Home—wherever that may be for you—probably set in motion the conditions that led to where you are today. Who contributed to your success? Who helped you prepare for today? Why not pick up the phone and make a quick call. Just say thank you to those who deserve it.

"Only you are responsible for you."   Once we realize that we have the ultimate responsibility for who we are, what we have, and how we live, we are able to move to the next level. Stop blaming others. Take responsibility for every part of your life. Your future is in your hands. Make sure you treat this opportunity responsibly.

"Just say no!"   Just say "no" to drugs, stereotypes, prejudice, discrimination, abusive relationships and violence. Say "no" to all the things we know are detrimental to us. What a simple, yet profound, way to think. Stop being subtle and say "no."

"Commit yourself to quality."   Why be satisfied with just doing okay, when you have the potential for high-quality living? Why would anyone be okay with simply getting by? Put positive energy out there, so you have positive energy from which to draw. Passivity leads to passivity. Action leads to improvement. Step it up a notch or two. Commit yourself to quality in all that you do.

"Avoid negative people."   Remember your grandmother's teaching—you'll become the people you hang around with! When you surrounded yourself with negatives, you will become negative. When you surround yourself with positives, you become more positive. Likewise, if you hang out with those who eat too much, you will eat more than normal; with those who drink too much, you will drink more than you should; with those who use foul language, you will add foul words to your vocabulary. Avoid negative people! Life is too short. Don't let those who are negative bring you down with them.

"Be prepared to lose once in awhile."   The road to the top often includes a few setbacks. The simple concept of challenge prepares you for the next curve. Losing is not a bad thing if you know how to respond to the loss. When you are prepared to lose, you are more likely to cherish the lessons you learned from your mistakes. Disappointment is a teachable moment.

"Count your blessings." Even in the worst times of your life, there's always value in counting your blessings. Be thankful for the opportunity of another day. Be thankful for the challenges you will face as they will provide opportunities to grow for tomorrow. Be thankful for those with whom you share your time as they help you grow and move toward progress. Be thankful for the air you breathe, for the sights you see, for the aromas you smell and for the things you feel. When you go to bed, end the day acknowledging things for which you can be thankful. It will help you prepare for another exciting tomorrow.

Powerful words with powerful meanings. Powerful statements by which we all should live our lives. It doesn't take much, just a word or two.

Rick Barnes

YOU ARE NEVER
NOT COMMUNICATING

Even when you say nothing at all, you are still communicating! Do you realize the number of non-verbal cues you are sending to those around you just by the way you stand, by your gestures and facial expressions? You are never not communicating.

Think about your posture. When you sit in a chair, do you slouch? Do you put your head in your hands? This tells people you are tired, or having a bad day. Do you fold your arms? That tells people you're closed off—you don't want to communicate right now. But that signal itself is a form of communication.

When you smile at people, you say "I notice you." When you look right through people, you say "you don't matter to me right now." A raised eyebrow suggests you're intrigued; a furrowed brow could mean you're confused. A subtle grin may be a shared joke. Silence speaks volumes.

Do you maintain eye contact with people when you speak to them? Many interpret eye contact as a sign of trustworthiness. If you are not looking someone directly in the eye, you must be hiding something. Do you listen actively when others speak to you? Do you nod to show you understand them? If you don't show others that you are listening to them, why should they listen to you?

Be aware of non-verbal communication. Actions speak louder than words. Imagine the advantage if you are looking for non-verbal cues, and others aren't. Realize that you are always communicating—even when you're *not* saying anything!

Judson Laipply

YOU TO THEM

Them to you or me to you...
We communicate.

One to one, one on one or
to absolutely no one else but ourselves...
We communicate.

Fax to fax, face to face,
Mail to e-mail, male to female, friend to foe,
student to student, or teacher to pupil...
We communicate.

Freely, firmly, formally, casually, calmly or urgently...
We communicate.

Over the internet, over the phone,
Over seas, over coffee, over a candlelit dinner, or
Over worked and under paid...
We communicate.

Under the weather, under the first amendment,
unintentionally, unprepared or unfortunately...
We communicate.

In rhythm, in time,
In control, or out of control,
out of necessity, or out of our minds...
    We communicate.

We strive to talk the walk and walk the talk,
Be who we say we are and say the right things,
all with an open heart, a generous soul and giving spirit.

You to them, them to you,
Me to you, one to one, one on one, or
to no one else but ourselves...
    We communicate.

Nancy Hunter Denney

Family

A MOTHER'S TOUCH

For all your impressions on me...
    Your faith to spread the spirit of God;
    Your smile to leave with others;
    Your kindness to capture hearts;
    Your eyes to see the good;
    And your light to enrich the earth.

For before I was me, there was you...
    Proud you are my mom;
    Grateful to be your child;
    And thankful my heart has been shaped by your touch.

Patti Geib Holmes

CONSTANT PRESENCE

I remember the day my grandmother passed away. I had just completed my master's degree and couldn't wait to tell her in person. Words of congratulations (and maybe even a little anticipated praise) were exchanged for devastating news. This ever constant presence in my life was gone.

No funeral is easy and this was no exception. After the service, what seemed like an endless stream of friends, neighbors and acquaintances came to the house to express their condolences. At first, I sat in solitude only slightly aware of the faint buzz of voices around me. I could hear bits and pieces of chatter, but I wasn't really listening—I was thinking about my grandmother.

A strikingly beautiful woman, my grandmother wore stylish clothes and had a loving smile. She was an extraordinary person who had the gift of making each of her grandchildren feel as though they were the most loved of all. When my parents went out of town, it was grandmother who stayed with us. She loved family celebrations. Every Christmas she took pride in her homemade eggnog, every birthday she showed off her caramel cakes and every holiday my grandmother gave all of her ten grandchildren checks!

Looking back on it, I wasn't ready for my grandmother to die. I was 24 years old and still needed her wisdom, company, and perspective on life. As I sat quietly thinking about special moments with my grandmother, I heard her name. Someone nearby was talking about my grandmother. It must have been a funny story because complete strangers were laughing in the kitchen. I began to listen more attentively and what unfolded were bits and pieces of her entire life—not just the parts I knew and lived.

She had dreams. She had traveled. She had a life before becoming my grandmother. That afternoon I met my grandmother as a complete person for the first time and saw sides of her I had never imagined.

My grandmother had nine siblings! She was the constant care taker (or nanny) to her youngest sister, and frequently played parent to the other eight. Despite her responsibilities at home, my grandmother excelled at school and earned straight A's. I had never even thought of her as a teenager, but she was apparently a brilliant dancer and swimmer in high school. Why hadn't I really looked at her before?

It turns out my grandmother didn't always have grey hair either! In her youth, she was said to have been a real beauty and highly pursued by every boy in town (and not all successfully.) Despite all of her potential suitors, there was one who captured her heart—my grandfather!

Although her parents highly disapproved of their courtship (he was ten years older,) my grandmother fell in love with her true soul mate at the age of fifteen. He was ten years older than she and divorced. Determined to be together, they abided by her father's rules and waited until she was eighteen to date, and twenty to marry. From what I was hearing, they were madly in love and being together was all that mattered. They were a match made in Heaven.

My grandfather was a doting husband and had many talents. He toured with the USO during World War II as an accomplished violinist and my grandmother performed with him as a dancer. Together they entertained the soldiers.

As years passed, the number of their joint adventures grew. I had never known they wrote famous children's songs together or how my grandfather supported her as she became a respected dance teacher, earned a teaching certificate (an unusual thing for women to do back then,) and raised two girls and a boy (my father.)

When my grandfather became ill with cancer, my grandmother was his hope and inspiration. Her deep dedication and love for her husband motivated her to do whatever she could to ease his pain. Cancer treatments weren't as sophisticated as they are today, so my grandmother had sought any means—including importing experimental medicines from Mexico. She was by his side when he died.

The time came when the laughter quieted and the stories ended. I believe they ended because it was getting late, not because there was a shortage of adventures or memories. As the last person shut the door behind him I stood stunned and speechless. How could I not have known all those things about my grandmother? Who was this woman who lived a lifetime before we met?

It occurred to me at some point later in the evening, I was the one who had chosen to see my grandmother not for the woman she was—but, as my grandmother and nothing else. I had chosen to interact with her based upon my needs. How I regret not shifting the focus (and spotlight) back on her—even if for a moment. Then, I came to another realization; my grandmother enjoyed her role as grandmother. Those other lives were for other times. The only regrets were mine for not knowing her as well as I could have.

Before I went to sleep I thought about all of the day's events. No funeral is easy. But this day brought a roller coaster of emotion—including complete joy in the life that had been my grandmother's before I knew her. I closed my eyes and thought about all of the stories I had heard one more time. I smiled and pleasant memories swirled through my head. Slight regret also flowed through my awareness before I drifted off to sleep. The day was finally over.

How well do we really know the people we love? My grandmother's life taught me the importance of getting to know the people in our life—including their childhoods, talents and dreams from their youth. Why wait until someone is gone to discover who they were? Why hear all the details from anyone other than the main character? Get the story of someone's life from the person who lived it.

Elaine Penn

INTO YOUR LIFE THEY COME

"To laugh often and much; to win the respect of intelligent people and the affection of children; to earn the appreciation of honest critics and endure the betrayal of false friends; to appreciate beauty, to find the best in others; to leave the world a little better; whether by a healthy child, a garden patch or a redeemed social condition; to know even one life has breathed easier because you have lived. This is the meaning of success."

\- *Ralph Waldo Emerson*

Looking at my twelve month old wearing a bowl of spaghetti like a hat, I wondered if life could get any better. Instead of rushing to clean up the mess, water down the stains on his green corduroy overalls, or wipe spaghetti off the walls, I simply watched with joy as my little guy played with his new hat and giggled. His face, arms, legs and hands were a beautiful Marinara color. Pasta hung from his ears. As fast as a six month pregnant mother-to-be could run, I found the camera to capture this moment.

There is something special about your first born child. Is it because they teach you unexpected things about yourself no one else can teach you? Into your life they come to share God's love and make you forever different. The three most important lessons I've learned from being a mother include: your capacity to love is endless; you need them more than they need you, and you always have time now.

Endless Love. Two months before my son was born a big fat raccoon started a nightly ritual of peeking through our bedroom window just around the start of my favorite show; Jake and the Fat Man. Using the oak tree next to our front porch as her egress, the raccoon would drop to the roof, scurry up the tiles, and then peek from a safe distance into our front bedroom window.

At first I was alarmed—after all, this wild (and potentially rabid) "peeping coon" might break through the glass and attack us during our sleep! Soon thereafter, I found her visits comforting and came to believe my masked companion was checking up on me. I could sense she sympathized with my growing discomfort, and possibly my husband's need for comfort of any kind.

The night I went into labor was my husband's birthday. We had gone out to dinner to celebrate. I still had three weeks to go, so we made it an early evening. The eternal optimist in me had ordered lobster because I had heard sea food can speed up a due date. Apparently, there is some truth to this myth. Before midnight, I was waking my husband to the alarming shrill, "It's time!"

Anticipating the chaos of the next year of his life, my husband leisurely strolled in his birthday suit down our small apartment's hallway to take a shower. I began timing my contractions as he shaved, lathered and rinsed his hair. By twelve thirty, I had read the last chapter of *What to Expect When You're Expecting* three times. Not knowing what to do next, I went into the nursery to make sure all was in order. There in the window was my friend, the raccoon.

She was much closer to the glass than she'd ever come before, way past her normal visiting hours, and at a completely different window. I wobbled my way to the rocking chair by the window and dropped into the seat. Looking into the masked brown eyes of the raccoon a calmness fell over me. Maybe it was the incredible beauty of the raccoon or the distraction, but for the first time I felt ready to become a mother. As my husband helped me out of the rocking chair, I said to my companion of the last half hour, "Here we go!"

My husband responded, "Yup, here we go!"

I looked over at the raccoon and winked. We knew I hadn't

been talking to my husband! That was the last I'd see of my companion—apparently, her work was done. Three hours later, my son was born.

It was almost 11 PM before everyone had finally left my room and I was alone with my baby for the first time. Jacob lay in my arms wearing a white cap tied with a baby blue string. His forehead was still black and blue, and his brown eyes never strayed from my eyes. Inches from my face he just stared at me as if I were his entire world. I felt my heart grow and thought; so this is the miracle called life—this is God's great power on earth.

Having It All. When my son was three months old, I went back to working full time. For some mothers, this is a difficult yet necessary choice. For others, it is a welcomed break from diapers and housecleaning—a chance to have an intellectual conversation. And, for some, a need to continue the life they had prior to having a baby. For me, going back to work was all part of an earlier subscription to living other people's definition of "having it all." My heart was broken, but I listened to my head.

For the months that followed, I ignored the unanticipated pain of leaving my baby in child care and missing all "the firsts." Being told of Jacob's first steps wasn't the same as seeing them. Other's attempts to comfort me with silly logic about "quality of time" did little to make me feel complete. Reminding me of my professional preparation or how my feelings of separation would eventually subside also did little to fix what was broken. Who was I kidding?

Every day became more and more of a struggle between my head and my heart. No wonder learning I was pregnant again came as a mixed blessing—now I'd have twice as much guilt, conflict and heartbreak!

On July 4th, fifteen months after the birth of my first baby, my daughter was born. Along with the fireworks came a sparkling revelation: I needed to be around my children more than they needed to be around me. The hole in my heart was only going to be filled by spending "quantity time" with my children. Something in my life needed to change—maybe it was me!

After considerable prayer and support from my husband, I recognized in my attempt to "have it all," I had nothing at all. Who-ever wrote the rules got them wrong. I thought about the night my son was born, the raccoon in my window, and how natural it felt to love my children. Allowing my heart to direct my decision making, I decided to quit my job and let my head figure out a way to work out of my home. Before long, all the pieces fell into place and de-spite having considerably less financially—as a family we had much more. Why did it take me so long to figure this out?

Time Now. I watched with horror from my hotel room at the television coverage of the Oklahoma City bombings the day before. My children were three and four years old now and the thought of losing them was beyond comprehension. My consulting work had taken me to Schenectady, NY, for two days and I wasn't sure how I was going to emotionally re-group after witnessing such a tragedy unraveling in front of me.

The image of a mother holding her little boy's white fluffy ted-dy bear on her lap has stayed present in my mind to this day. The mother looked directly into the camera and lovingly spoke of her son. She mentioned their conversation the night before he was killed. He wanted her to read him just one more bedtime story.

With remarkable composure the mother ended her story by saying, "I took the time and granted his wish. I'm so glad I took the time instead of rushing downstairs to do the dishes and pick up the house."

My children are now in high school and the countdown to col-lege is ever present in my mind. Instead of focusing on the "firsts" I find myself counting the "third to lasts." Accepting that you can't get time back is a powerful source of inspiration, and the one gift I wish I had allowed myself to open much earlier in my professional career. Why was I waiting for permission to be happy and present for my children?

Sure, my house isn't as clean as it could be, the dish wash-er doesn't always get unloaded, and I usually miss the last fifteen minutes of a show—but, into my life they came and my priorities changed—so I make (and take) the time to honor my daughter's nightly request to tuck her in, despite all I should be doing.

I don't return phone calls as quickly as my colleagues, submit enough articles for publication in all the "right" magazines, or stick around after speaking engagements to have dinner with people— but, into my life they came and it just doesn't seem to matter as much as it once did. I've changed. Taking the kids rock climbing at the YMCA, teaching my own children about life and being around more, not less, in their teenage years is where I feel most satisfied, happy and successful. This is what works for me.

In addition, all cell phones (including mine) go off in the car so we can turn on a conversation. Preparing dinner doesn't take as long as sitting down and having dinner, and being around is much more meaningful than running around. Motherhood (or parenting) is a one shot deal and if I mess this up, I don't get a "do-over."

Before long I will go upstairs and walk by two rooms currently occupied by my teenagers—each with a different style of music blaring, and a week's worth of wardrobe on the floor. It's only a matter of time before my daughter stops asking me to tuck her in at night, and my son begins to prefer his friends over his mother to go rock climbing. But today they are asking, so today I am granting their wishes. Why not honor my children on their time?

In the End. They say there's something special about your first born—and there is, but there's something special about all the people in your life. God created us to love us. God wants us to love one another by sharing our best—not our exhausted, overextended and short tempered selves. He also wants us to love ourselves enough to follow our hearts. For within your heart lies an incredible capacity to love, a wonderful guide for making the tough decisions in life, and the understanding time is something you can't take back!

Nancy Hunter Denney

WHAT'S THE SCOOP?

A few months before my brother passed away, he asked me to promise that I would spend Father's Day with his two sons. He asked me to remind them that they had a father who would always love them. Of course I said I would. This was a promise I was determined to keep.

The first Father's Day after my brother's death, his boys wanted to go for ice cream. They asked for Ben and Jerry's, rather than the local shop that was much closer. I explained that this local shop was more convenient, but the boys insisted. After a few minutes of debate, I relented. With a Happy Father's Day balloon in my hand, I set off with my brother's boy to enjoy Cherry Garcia.

We ordered our ice cream, and when I went to pay for the cones, the clerk said, "Yours is free today because every father gets a free ice cream on Father's Day."

I looked at my two beaming nephews, and realized why they wanted to go to Ben and Jerry's. Holding back tears, I joined my nephews at the ice cream counter. I was quickly learning the power of parenthood.

Even at age six and eight, these boys knew how to make me feel special. They showed their very appreciative "bruncle" (a "bruncle" is when you combine a brother and uncle) that he mattered to them very much.

Remember that you matter to the people in your life. For every person who's touched your life in a meaningful way, think of the ways you recognize them. Realize that you can make a difference simply by being there, with tokens of expression as simple as an ice cream cone. Who matters to you? How do they know they matter to you?

My brother's boys taught me a valuable lesson about mattering—about simple expressions of appreciation and love. I smile just thinking of the happiness fathers share, knowing how special they are to their sons and daughters. I think about the kindness of my brother's boys, and the love they show me, their "bruncle."

In January of 2006, a few Father's Days later, I opened a gelato shop in Florida called "What's the Scoop?" Our slogan is "a little dish never hurt anyone." This line of work enables me to celebrate and share some small moments of mattering with others every day. And you can be sure, on Father's Day, I'll put a sign in my shop window: "FREE cones for Fathers!" Father's Day cannot get here soon enough.

Doug Cureton

Life

A MEANINGFUL LIFE

Everyone experiences an "ah-ha" moment or two in life. The "ah-ha" moments represent that pivotal point, or clarity beyond belief, forcing you to finally own your behaviors and attitudes. They represent that remarkable time in history when you realize it's time to face your reality—the good, bad and unimaginable. You wake up knowing it wasn't a dream; you are where you are because of the choices you have made.

Some "ah-ha" moments are more fun than others. Some bring you relief, others acceptance. Some bring you inner peace, others the ability to forgive. Some end chapters in your life, while others make you want to rip out the pages of your life story. Some force you to decide between a wasted life, or one lived with purpose. It is through "ah-ha" moments you come to terms with life itself.

A few years after graduating from college, I awoke not knowing where I was, how I got there, or who I was with. It had been a wild evening, given the extent of my hang over. My "just want to have fun" behaviors as an undergraduate had followed me into real life, including the potentially disastrous consequences of such irresponsible behavior. With my head ready to split open, I had an "ah-ha" moment. I decided to quit drinking immediately.

Shortly thereafter, I began to experience what it really felt like to be healthy and happy. I was free to enter relationships based on a building attraction, common interests and mutual respect. I was taking care of myself, making responsible decisions and enjoying life.

In an instant, my life changed. As I left the doctor's office, I was forced to accept that my past had become my future. The HIV test came back positive. On the way to my car, I had to stop and catch my breath, and experienced another "ah-ha" moment. As I was walking around the block, I noticed flowers, a deep blue sky, and the smell of summer. Before this, I didn't know summer even had a smell. My closest encounters with nature, prior to this experience, had always been reading an L.L. Bean catalog.

With awakened senses and heightened awareness, I decided that I would never take another moment of my life for granted. I also didn't sleep much. In fact, many sleepless nights followed my diagnosis. I spent hours channel-surfing and looking for ways to take my restless mind off my situation.

One night, I happened upon the movie Wall Street. The main character is a guy whose life comes crashing down around him because of the poor choices he had made. I could relate. A friend ultimately saves the actor with the following advice: "Man looks into the abyss, there's nothing staring back at him. At that time a man finds his character—and that is what keeps him out of the abyss."

If only I was reading a script. That night I realized I was looking at my personal abyss. If I was going to survive my situation, I had to find my character. I wanted to be defined as someone who could take dark clouds, embrace them, and make room for the light. This was the "ah-ha" moment that saved my life.

In the months to follow, I had plenty of time to reflect upon how I had arrived at this place. My college days were filled with too many parties, too much alcohol, and unchecked behaviors. The more I remembered, the more disturbed I became. Despite all the out of classroom education I got on "hot topics," I couldn't recall hearing anyone connect alcohol use and the spread of infections or sexually transmitted diseases. I wanted my diagnosis to mean something. I needed to make a difference. My life was going have a purpose: I would work to bring this connection to the forefront.

My grade in college speech class was a pitiful "C." Not too

impressive. To say I was terrified of public speaking was an understatement. I wasn't exactly rushing to the podium, yet was passionate about sharing my story and wanted to help others make better choices than I had made in college. I now knew the only way to overcome my fear was to face it head-on. I decided to speak to whoever would listen.

Soon, the podium found me. I was asked to share my story at a university in Texas. After coaching and support from a friend, I found the words and courage to warn young adults of the harmful consequences of irresponsible sexual behavior caused by drinking too much. My audience and I shared the common bond of alcohol abuse. As I candidly related my experiences, admitted my mistakes and dared to confront my behaviors without question, I became free again.

Shortly thereafter, I had another "ah-ha" moment: I wanted to launch an innovative educational program called "Friendship in the Age of AIDS." The program took off like wildfire. In one city, the story of my program actually ran ahead of President Clinton's visit to town on the evening news! More important, hundreds of thousands of young adults were learning how HIV doesn't discriminate based on age, gender, ethnicity, or anything else.

I wonder frequently if my "ah-ha" moments will save others. I know they have saved me. But the thing about these moments is you don't always get to take credit for them. You don't always create them. My life has taught me that when you least expect it, someone or something reveals the purpose behind a previous "ah-ha" moment. You get to acknowledge that the purpose of your life is meaningful to you, and others.

Jared was a college freshman. He had just pledged a fraternity. After my program, Jared shared with me that he too was HIV-positive. He said he didn't want to keep the truth from his new brothers and friends in the fraternity. I appreciated Jared's conflicting emotions and during our conversation, he asked, "Do you think I will be accepted if people know the truth about me, about my HIV status?" I gave him some advice, then responded, "No two experiences are the same."

Jared listened intently, thanked me and gave me a hug. Before he left, I said, "Sleep on it. Remember, no two experiences are the same." On his way out the door, Jared turned and said, "I wish more than twenty-five students had been here tonight. There are twenty-five thousand on campus." I gave Jared my contact information, assured him our conversation had meaning to me, and wished him well.

Almost a year later I found myself back at Jared's university. I wondered if he had anything to do with the invitation and hoped to hear how his new found friendships had responded to his disclosure, if in fact he had taken that path.

Much to my delight, I learned that this courageous young man's friendships were just that—true friendships. As individuals, and as a fraternity organization, Jared's friends had embraced him. Much to my heartbreak, I also learned that my program that evening was going to begin with a "white rose" ceremony. Jared had died of AIDS the night before my arrival and his chapter wanted to honor his life.

Three thousand students showed up to hear the message Jared wanted them to hear; that is, my message. As each fraternity brother laid a white rose on stage, Jared and I shared another "ah-ha" moment. Our lives are changing other lives. That particular night everyone present understood our message: AIDS is part of our world.

I am where I should be. I am living my life with meaning and purpose. There is much work to be done. In the year 2006, HIV is at an all time high among young adults between the ages of fourteen and twenty-four in the United States, with fifty percent of all new cases coming from this age group. There is much work to be done.

When I begin to question whether young adults are listening, or if all of the "ah-ha" moments in my life really happened, I go into my wallet and pull out the following George Bernard Shaw quote. It reminds me that I am exactly where I should be.

"This is the true joy in life, the being used for a purpose recognized by yourself as a mighty one; the being thoroughly worn out before you

are thrown on the scrap heap; the being a force of nature instead of a feverish, selfish, little clod of ailments and grievances, complaining that the world will not devote itself to making you happy. I am of the opinion that my life belongs to the whole community, and as long as I live it is my privilege to do for it whatever I can. I want to be thoroughly used up when I die, for the harder I work the more I live. I rejoice in life for its own sake. Life is no 'brief candle' to me. It is a sort of splendid torch which I have got hold of for a moment, and I want to make it burn as brightly as possible before handing it on to future generations."

Joel A. Goldman

COMMANDMENTS FOR A
LIFE WORTH LIVING

Love yourself enough to do what you love.
Do what you would do if you knew you wouldn't fail.
Decide to trust—then trust your decision.
Move the ladder you're climbing against the right wall.
Stop wondering if it's an excuse—it's an excuse.
Recognize every moment is the moment of truth.
Develop courage by doing courageous things.
Resist the temptation to resist change.
Choose your actions carefully—they become your life.

Gary Tuerack

FINDING HAPPINESS

Happiness! We're all after it, but what is it? Where does it come from? How can we obtain it and hold on to it? Why does it seem to be so fleeting, coming and going throughout our lives? Why can't we choose to be happy all the time rather than just part of the time? We ask ourselves these questions every day, but simply asking is not enough! We want answers, and we want them right now!

Americans live in a paradox. Many are fortunate to have stable jobs and steady incomes, loving relationships and families, and material pleasures. We are a privileged society. From the outside looking in, for many Americans, life is good.

At the same time, people are empty on the inside and spiritually hungry. Charles Dickens described the American predicament in a *Tale of Two Cities: "It was the best of times, it was the worst of times, it was the age of wisdom, it was the age of foolishness, it was the epoch of belief, it was the epoch of incredulity, it was the season of light, it was the season of darkness, it was the spring of hope, it was the winter of despair, we had everything before us, we had nothing before us, we were all going direct to Heaven, we were all going direct the other way."*

Yes! The American Dream might just be life's greatest paradox. Ask yourself: Do all the material things you possess in this world bring you true happiness? Could you actually have more by having less? If everything designed to give you happiness still makes you feel empty inside, could happiness be inaccurately defined?

Discussing happiness can be somewhat depressing! The very topic can bring to the surface the realities of life which we hide beneath our material possessions and surface "success." What is happiness?

I struggle with what it means to be happy because, like you, I have a story.

Many believe happiness is having the financial means to live comfortably, not having to struggle to make ends meet. I suppose this is true. Yet, I still know plenty of people with lots of money who are miserable!

Theologian William Barclay said you need three things to be happy in life: "Someone to love, something to do, and something to look forward to." This seems to be a popular theme, appearing hundreds of different ways when you take the time to "google" the phrase, "the secret of happiness," along with the definitions "happiness is appreciating what you have," and "happiness is a choice you make."

Of the thousands of definitions of happiness I've explored, the most consistent factor is always the word "you." Apparently, you are the only one who can answer, or define, the happiness you will—or won't—experience. After pondering the question of happiness for some time, I conclude the "secret" to happiness isn't really a secret, at all. Happiness is simply the investment you put into you! What parts of you? Your faith, family and friends. Mystery solved.

Faith. "Faith is the assurance of things hoped for, the conviction of things not seen." (Hebrews 11:1)

Understanding true faith can be difficult. I know. One of my favorite authors, Frederick Buechner, makes it easy: "Faith is better understood as a verb rather than a noun. It is on-again-off-again rather than once-and-for-all. Faith is not being sure where you're going but going anyway. It is a journey without maps." It's easy to say you have faith, but if you don't practice or live it, how serious is the faith you profess? Faith must become something you do, not just something you claim to possess.

During his life and ministry, Christ talked and taught faith. When asked about the greatest commandment—what is it that which we are called to do first and foremost in life, Christ said: "Love God with all your heart, soul, and mind" (Matthew 22:37). How do you truly love God? What does it mean to love God day to day?

Through Christ, we know that the essence of God is love. We know God calls us to live in community with one another and to spread that love to others through acts of service. People desperately seek community, looking for a place to belong. They want what you want—to be loved and cared about. They want what you want—to have spiritual and emotional abundance. God calls us to reach out and share our life with others. We are rewarded when we learn to love others as Christ loved, and to put others' needs ahead of our own.

The great educator and theologian Martin Buber said, "All of us realize that we need God, but what we must also come to understand is that God needs us." True faith is helping God spread love to a hurting world, one which is closer than you think. Show your faith in your actions, and in how you treat others. Learn to surrender your life to the one who created it.

Family. Family is a place in the heart. You can create a family where there is none by connecting to one or more people who accept you for who you are—no conditions, tests or applications. Just you. Whether a phone call once a week, drop by visit, meal, or spiritual connection, the love of family doesn't have to come from two biological parents, or siblings. You can seek and find joy when you accept many of the loving relationships in your life as being with your "family."

I once heard: "Family is where you find refuge and security in a stormy world, and there are all kinds of storms in life. Family is where you can be yourself, where those who love you accept you as you are with no need for pretenses. Family is where you are always welcome no matter what. The world can and does reject you in many ways, but your family will always love you."

I am blessed with a father, sister and two brothers who I love very much. As a pastor, I recognize not everyone has this kind of warmth and unconditional regard of family, or the kind seen on television commercials around the holidays. Some families are downright dysfunctional or non-existent. Some families value time away from one another over time together, never truly appreciating what they have had until it is too late. How tragic, when pride, unresolved conflicts and pettiness are given more power than God's love.

If you seek happiness, start expressing your appreciation to your family. Reach out and let them know you think of them! Send a card. Take care of them. Hug. Pray for them. Call or e-mail or text message... reach out and touch! Although busy lives make it hard for us to spend time around the dinner table discussing family values, traditions and morals, you must make the time! Turn off the television, say "no" to activities pulling you away from your home, and FOCUS ON FAMILY! Make family meals a priority at least five nights a week. When you fail to touch base and check in, family members (especially teenagers) begin to check out.

Last year, I lost my Mother. I am in my twenties. Not a day goes by that I don't think of her, or wish I could just sit and have a conversation with her—just one more time. Why do people let time with loved ones slip by? Do you? Do you spend so much time trying to please others that you forget about those who deserve your best? When you put family first—whoever that is for you, God will rejoice.

Friends. Learning the importance of having and keeping friends (much like family) is the third secret to being happy in life. Nothing can replace true friends, or old friends.

"Two are better than one... for if one falls, the other will lift him up." (Ecclesiastes 4: 9-10)

It can be difficult to find true friendship, but I believe having one person who you call "friend" leads to happiness more than having many false friends. A true friend will forgive your failures, praise your accomplishments, build you up, and bring you joy. Friends are there for you whether you ask them to show up or not, never asking for anything in return. Even when the world turns its back on you, a friend remains.

Making good friends requires you to be a good friend. Act out of love, not jealousy. Give, don't take. Worship and cherish your friends, and in return you will be blessed.

What is the secret to being happy? In the New Testament, we read the parable of the wise and foolish builder in the seventh chapter of Matthew. Christ tells of the man who built his house on rock and how it was able to withstand the storms of life because it was built on rock. He also tells of the man who built his house on sand and when the storms of life blew, its weak foundation caused it to fall.

Build your precious life on the three things that matter most: faith, family and friends, things money can't buy, but last an eternity.

Rev. Clay Stauffer

GETTING MORE
OUT OF LIFE

If you want to live an extraordinary life, if you want to experience extraordinary moments, you must take extraordinary actions.

Are there things you want to do in this world, experiences you long to have, or goals you desire to achieve? If so, why is it you find yourself tangled, mangled, and caught up? Why do you keep living the same life—over and over again? Paralyzed from moving forward, you wake to the "same old same old." Don't panic... you're not alone!

Humans are creatures of habit. We get into routines. We have our set ways of living, acting and responding to the world around us. We get trapped in living out of habit, acting merely out of years of conditioning, rather than living the way we wished we were living. We stay in our "comfort zone"—the place where you know what you know, and often avoid new experiences or the unknown. The "comfort zone" protects us from uncertainty—guaranteeing sameness, staleness, settling and safety. Nothing ever changes when everything stays the same in this zone of comfort.

In order for something (or someone) to change, something (like an attitude, action, belief or response) needs to shift. To break free from your habits, you will need to literally take action, make a move and alter the manner in which you have been spending your time. You must push past your conditioned way of responding to others, making decisions, and working towards your goals. You can't expect different results by repeating the same behaviors. It's time to establish new habits!

The first step in changing your habits is to see yourself in a different way—a better way. Because one of the strongest psychological drives of human behavior is to maintain our self-built identity, to break habits (or move out of your "comfort zone") means you have to create an identity consistent with how you want to be and what you want out of life.

Start by asking yourself the following questions:

What do I want?

What will make me (even) happier?

What is missing in my life?

Why aren't I willing to allow myself to be happy?

What actions keep me stuck?

What five goals do I want to achieve this month?

Every time you continue to act the way you've been acting, you strengthen that particular habit or pattern of thinking. You have technically subtracted from your potential for a better you. The way to move forward begins by thinking forward. Every day you can make a new decision. So, which do you want to rule your life—those things that matter to you (like your dreams, desired relationships, health and potential success) or your habits? What new decision are you going to make today?

After seeing yourself differently, the next step to changing your habits is to understand the unproductive and false thinking patterns around trying something new. Specifically, at the root of the problem is the human tendency to link feelings with actions—we think we have to feel like doing something in order to do it.

If we don't feel like starting up an exercise program for ourselves, we often delay the actions needed to begin. If we don't feel like quitting smoking, we don't visit our doctor, get the prescription, or go to the cessation program. We tell ourselves, "I'll wait until I feel ready." With this pattern of thinking, you'll never actually do anything new.

To start new habits, start doing new behaviors—whether you feel like it or not! Starting a new diet, for example, never really feels right. Beginning a new exercise routine, never really feels right. Trying to mend a bad relationship by talking things through, never really feels right. All of these can be down right painful! If you wait to take action until you feel like it, you may end up standing still.

So, what do you want? What actions do you need to be conditioned or re-conditioned to do on a regular basis? What will lead to the achievement of your goals? Force yourself to do what it takes to add to your future. You may think small steps (like ten minutes of walking instead of staying at your desk) don't add up, but they do. Accept the fact any change may be uncomfortable, inconvenient, hard and painful in the beginning—do what it takes anyway. If you need to enlist a friend, deadline or hire someone to keep you on task, then that's what you need to do. Invest in you.

Nothing worth achieving comes without conscious effort, and nothing new comes without doing something new!

Gary Tuerack

LIFE BY DESIGN

L ife is a place, a state of mind, and a period in time.
It's the sun waiting to rise, the certainty and the surprise.

Life is where you reside, sing, dance, run, seek and hide.
It's the framing of your soul, a spirit within a goal.

Life is the ups and downs, achievements, failures, smiles and frowns.
It's the passions you pursue, a truth to see through.

Life is not what you pass by, trade up, settle for or deny.
It's the acceptance of growth, a journey of faith and hope.

Life is the sailboat still on anchor, knowing the wind will soon sail
her.
It's the legacy of your being, a destiny worth seeing.

So, live your life for it is real, risk it all, reach high and feel.
Build a dream that's one of a kind, a place to call home, a life by
design.

Nancy Hunter Denney

LIFE LESSONS FROM ONE HUNDRED LOST

"Less really is *more."*

Ilost one hundred pounds. After spending most of my life as an overweight person—a chubby kid, big teenager, and fat man, I finally realized that losing weight involved the same lessons I had learned about living a successful life. The secret to getting fit, as it turns out, wasn't a secret at all. In fact, it was no different from anything else I was doing to achieve goals in other parts of my life. I just needed to apply them to my physical well-being.

Does this sound familiar: When my weight gets in my way, I will take care of it? That time finally came. My weight was "in my way" physically and more importantly, mentally. Once I accepted what had to be done, I got serious and did it. Whatever you want to do—whether you want to lose weight, get in better shape, learn a new language, or run a marathon—you can do it! My life is a testimony to potential willpower and success.

Success in one aspect of your life carries over to all the other areas. When you make a plan and follow it, you get results. When you don't make a plan, nothing changes. Here's a list of life lessons which apply not only to losing weight, but to getting the most out of your life:

Know yourself. I ate a lot when I was fat—vegetable, chicken, and salads. I was a "volume eater." Through experience, and learning about nutrition, I learned that it's not liking to eat that made me fat, but rather what I ate! Once I acknowledged this, I was free to focus on eating the right foods. I was free to lose weight. I didn't waste time worrying and focusing on unproductive behaviors.

Isn't this how it is in other areas of your life? For example, say you believe that you're not good at math, but you are required to take a math class. You spend time worrying about how you'll even pass the class given your experience and track record. You spend time figuring out the minimum number of questions you'll need to get right in order to just pass the test, and the fewest concepts you'll need to understand in order to get by and "get it over with."

Afraid of appearing "stupid," you go so far as to avoid asking your teacher for help and you suffer in silence. Is it any wonder that you most likely are going to fail or get a poor grade? After all, you approached your goal trusting your past failures, instead of trusting your future success. You focused on how bad you are, not on your potential success or desired outcome.

To be successful, ask leading questions: *How can I raise my confidence? What am I really not understanding and how can I learn it better? Where do I freeze up and what strategies do I need to use to get un-frozen? Would extra time on certain concepts improve my results?* Answering these questions helps you know yourself. Acting on your answers without excessive doubt or worry not only demonstrates your self-confidence, it builds more confidences. Your chances for success are improved the moment you ask HOW you can achieve your goals, not IF you will achieve them!

Most of us learn about ourselves from others. We draw conclusions about our aptitudes, personality and potential based on our exchanges with others. As kids, we get direct feedback from other kids as well—whether we want it or not! If you were ever on the receiving end of an insult, or were politely dismissed after giving a class presentation, for example, you understand how easy it is to "own" the way others see you. In fact, you "own" it so well, you make it true.

For example, if you believe you aren't a good leader because someone might have suggested that to you in the past, do you buy into that assessment, or do you do what it takes to prove that person wrong? If you believe you aren't good in front of a group, do you avoid leading groups, speaking publicly and taking "up front" positions? If you act, however, on your own constructive self-knowledge and potential while accepting your weaknesses (i.e. organizational skills, public speaking skills, etc.) you are in a much better position to do what it takes to improve. Anyone can improve on anything! To better know yourself, start asking: *Why do I feel this way? How can I better prepare to meet obstacles? What skills should I learn to be a better leader?*

When I set out to lose one hundred pounds, I was not confident in my abilities. I had to stop looking at myself as I knew others saw me, and see myself as thin and fit. I had to get to know the real me, learn HOW to lose weight healthily, and believe it was possible. Once I did these things, my confidence also improved.

Stay focused and keep it simple. As a Bronx-raised American man, I believed anything was possible through hard work and the application of my talents. I was blessed with a wonderful view of the world: If anything is possible, I want it all! Unfortunately, having so many choices can be paralyzing.

Have you ever been overwhelmed after a stroll down the snack aisle at a supermarket? You end up leaving empty-handed because you can't make a selection. Baked or toasted, fat or nonfat, or low fat, super-sized or mini-sized, individual packets or jumbo, salted or lightly salted or salt free?

If you approach your weight loss, or any life goal, knowing in advance what you are trying to achieve, you will be less likely to be distracted, side-tracked or overwhelmed. Stay focused, spend time on your short-term objectives. Take small, manageable steps (i.e. run around the block three consecutive days before you sign up for a marathon!)

When I weighed three hundred pounds and had a forty-six inch waist (the largest size at most stores) it finally hit me—it was time to do something about my fitness! Given my "anything is possible" outlook on life, I decided to join a gym, work out regularly, and start a diet of some kind. Should it be low fat, low carb,

Weight Watchers, Atkins, or LA Weight Loss? Maybe a nutrition-ist would be helpful?

Wow! That's a lot of choices, especially when facing one of the most difficult goals I've ever set for myself. Can you imagine how easy it would have been to get lost in the details, and never focus enough to move toward action? To narrow my choices, I decided to seek my doctor's advice and learned something very valuable.

I needed to first build my confidence through a moderate amount of success at the scale before I jumped into joining a gym, buying the right workout clothes, paying gym fees, and so on. Wor-rying about exercise before I knew I could lose weight could poten-tially sabotage my success. So I found a diet program that worked for me and focused the first three months on losing weight.

Each day I became more confident in the program, as well my ability to lose weight. The next logical step was to begin exercis-ing. I started with an easy at-home video. Before I knew it, I was running outside. Next, I joined a gym. My steps turned into jogs, which became miles! By figuring out what was most important first, focusing on it, and simultaneously excluding other distrac-tions, I was achieving my goal. The same applies to any aspect of your life.

Accept the ups and downs before you begin. Even when you experience success, the road that got you there wasn't straight. The road to success is curved! My weight loss wasn't all down hill, either. That's just not how weight loss works. If you charted my weight loss on a graph, you would notice a steady decline over sixteen months. But, if you looked at it more closely, you'd see a rather jagged line with slight gains in the overall downward pat-tern.

When you have a goal in mind and are on your way to achiev-ing it, know setbacks (or jagged lines) are normal. Don't be dis-couraged by periods of difficulty, lost focus, or distractions. Deal with them and move on. Consider why they are happening and fix what's broken. Acknowledge your temporary setback as one stop on the road to success. Even if you slide backwards a bit, you are further ahead of where you began. Stay the course—your course.

Don't give up after a few set-backs. That will only ensure that you'll never get what you really want.

Enjoy difficulty. Even though something is difficult (like vacuuming an entire house) you can still enjoy it. While I was losing pound after pound, step after step, good food choice after good food choice, I began to realize that although this was work, it was also enjoyable. Not at first, of course, but once I accepted that my effort was paying off, exercising became more fun. I enjoyed feeling in control of my body. I experienced pleasure in the satisfaction of self-discipline.

Do you enjoy exercising? Maybe you would if you had more time. I understand all the reasons why not to enjoy exercise— it's work! You are expending energy from reserves which may or may not be there. Given the other priorities in your life, exercising might not be worth investing your time. When something is viewed as more fun and less work, though, we tend to choose that activity (i.e. watching three consecutive hours of television) over the harder one.

At three hundred pounds, I couldn't have imagined running a marathon. It was too hard. Running wasn't fun. When my attitude about exercising (and running in particular) changed, I found myself looking forward to the time when my feet would hit the street! Think about thinking differently. What goals could you achieve if you found pleasure and enjoyment in the process, instead of challenge?

I actually ran a half marathon not too long ago! The training was difficult. Every week a mile was added to my distance. It was work. One beautiful New England day, I found myself out for a run and decided not to measure the mileage. Off I went for an enjoyable couple of hours. It was grueling, exhausting and difficult. It was also great! I was having so much fun, I exceeded my half-marathon distance and ran fourteen miles. Why not enjoy the work you do to achieve your goals? Consider the alternative.

Keep doing what works. "Michael, this is terrific! All you need to do to lose weight is keep doing what you're doing!" said the person who weighed me in at Weight Watchers. This was a moment of transformation in my life. There was no secret or magic to achieving my weight loss goal. I just needed to be consistent—doing the right things over and over again.

Have you noticed the same philosophy applies to life? A financial advisor, for example, will tell you that if you put away consistent amounts of cash over a consistent period of time, you will earn more than "one shot" investments made too late in life. They aren't advising you to risk your retirement on "high-growth, high-risk" funds. Similarly, I'm not advising you to buy into a "lose ten pounds in ten days" program by taking some "magic formula." The lesson is simple—start doing what it takes to be successful, do it consistently, and keep doing it.

Whatever your goals, you can achieve them! I know this. Most people I meet struggle with some aspect of life—including weight loss. Extremely successful people in their professions, for example, also struggle with staying fit. This means they have decided to do what it takes in one area of their life to get what they want, but not in another area. How about you? Are you as successful as you want in all areas of your life, or does something need your attention? Inside of you is everything you need to begin tapping into your true capabilities!

Michael Miller

NO GUARANTEES

"Jimmy has collapsed at Discovery Zone with the boys," my mother said over the phone. I don't recall ever hearing her so somber, without her usual reassuring tone.

"Is he alright? Are the boys OK?" I asked.

"The boys are fine. Jimmy is still in the hospital. Something hemorrhaged and he fainted," my mother explained.

"Would you like me to come home now?" I asked, expecting the usual response of "No, everything will be fine."

Instead, a quiet voice on the other end of the line responded, "Yes. When can you get here?"

Later, in the hospital, the neurosurgeon asked Jimmy a number of questions. "Who is the president of the United States?" he quizzed.

From his bedside, my brother responded, "Bill Clinton." I smiled, reassured.

The neurosurgeon continued, "Do you know who the President was before Clinton?" Without hesitating, my brother answered, "Reagan?"

Many people make that mistake, I rationalized. Bush is easy to forget. The quiz continued: "How much is four times four?"

"Eight." said my brother.

The surgeon emphatically repeated his question, "Four times four equals what?"

This time, I could tell Jimmy was guessing. "Twelve?" My heart began to sink. Where was the Cureton family shield, which was supposed to protect us from the misfortune other families encountered?

The surgeon waved me out into the hallway, interrupting my thoughts. A nurse continued to attend to Jimmy as the doctor spoke with me. "A gliobastoma tumor is the worst possible tumor," he said. "Jimmy has six months—at the most. Make the most of the time. Make sure his life is in order."

Bracing myself against the door jam I asked, "Should we tell him?"

"That is up to you and your family," advised the surgeon. "In my opinion, it won't change the outcome and it will do nothing but dampen his spirit." I thanked the doctor for his honesty and started on the journey of saying goodbye to my brother.

While I was well-versed on the topic of stress management, none of the helpful models or mantras came to mind. Isn't it odd how the advice you skillfully espouse to others can fail you when you need it most? My thoughts were interrupted by my mother's voice: "This is the worst possible news we could have gotten." Her eyes held in tears she willed not to drop.

I looked back at my mother and softly said, "No. The worst news would have been if the tumor had hemorrhaged while he was driving the boys to the Discovery Zone. Then, we might not have the boys or the time we have now." Silence.

During the next six months, every picture we took had new importance. I preserved our conversations in my mind's archive, knowing they would lovingly serve me later. Time seemed to fly. Unfortunately, my brother's time did come. The doctors were accurate almost to the day.

"Sometimes people leave you halfway through the woods," I said in my eulogy. "Do not let it grieve you; no one leaves for good." Sondheim's lyrics seemed most fitting for a life gone too soon. They've rung particularly true for me. Even after his death, Jimmy could never really leave for good. He was there for the holidays, birthdays and family traditions. He was there.

Jimmy's fate had me thinking about my own life. What had I accomplished? I came to the conclusion that I wasn't guaranteed any time on this Earth, no more than my brother was.

Shortly after Jimmy's collapse in the Discovery Zone, I left my position with the Anti-Defamation League and returned home. I was determined to help take care of my brother. Jimmy once asked when I was returning to work. I lied and answered, "I'm being transferred to Florida, so there's some transition time while they set up the office." Even lies have some truth to them.

Some time after Jimmy's funeral, I moved to Florida. I realized that the quality of my life was up to me and me alone. Moving to Florida meant I was leaving my comfort zone, and challenging my sense of security. I jeopardized everything I had worked for up to that point.

My move to Florida was of my own choosing. I'm reminded of another Sondheim affirmation from Move On, "The choice may have been mistaken, the choosing was not."

As I drove down to Florida, a stream of what-ifs dashed through my mind, mile after mile. Jimmy's presence was palpable. I knew that if I didn't at least try to follow my passion, I would always wonder if I could have done it. I had to take the chance. There were no guarantees.

Shortly after arriving in Florida, I launched my leadership train-ing company, CreativiTEAM, which became successful on many fronts. I have been able to do the work I love, for people I respect, and in the time frame I choose. This leap of faith—sparked by my brother's untimely death—brought me to places I could never have imagined.

Complacency can feel great at first, but after a while, you start to realize that you aren't being challenged and your life isn't all that exciting. Eventually you confront the question: "This is it?"

Taking risks and opening up to new opportunities requires a sense of adventure. You must be willing to leave the "This is it?" zone. Life is a series of challenges that can lead you to one of two choices: success or failure. When you achieve a level of success and remain there because it's safe, have you actually succeeded? Or are you "nesting?"

Complacency may be an opportunity to turn unproductive

questions into the most productive question of all: "How can I help?" There will be a day when someone needs your time and talents.

Life is precious. You must seek out opportunities that will challenge you. You've got to interact with others who share your passion. Define and refine your skills. Then do it again. And most of all, you must believe in yourself. Do something with your life that matters to you. And, remember...there are no guarantees.

Doug Cureton

IT'S NOT ABOUT
THE DESTINATION

*"For a long time it seemed to me that life was about to begin—
real life, but there was always some obstacle in the way,
something to be gotten through first, some unfinished business,
time still to be served, a debt to be paid. At last it dawned on me
that these obstacles were my life. This perspective has helped me to see
there is no way to happiness. Happiness is the way. So treasure every
moment you have and remember that time waits for no one."*

- Souza

As a little child growing up in a small town in the southernmost
part of Louisiana, the world seemed so big and far away to me.
But I was a dreamer. I could imagine myself in amazing places.

My grandmother took me to those amazing places through stories and books. Together we imagined how incredible it would be
to visit Ireland, a Broadway play in the Big Apple, beautiful areas
with clouds circling distant mountains. My grandmother taught
me to imagine and dream. Then, she taught me to enjoy the ride.

I'm thankful for those days gone by, those days spent on the
river bank dreaming about the world and what possibilities lay in
front of me. I recognize now that my grandmother was teaching
me one of life's most important lessons: It is about the journey not
the destination, and to be truly happy, it's important to value those

reflective parts of your life that allow you to explore your true self.

Take a moment right now to think about all the twists and turns in your life. What did they teach you? For example, can you recall when certain things, like having the "right" clothes, or being in the "right" crowd was important? I bet these things don't mean as much to you today.

Think about the people who have come into your life and changed it forever. Who are they? Think about all of the stories you've heard and read. What impact have they made on your decision-making? If you live the best life you can now, and value each day as an important part of your journey, happiness will come to you. Said another way, if you are always living for the future, you can't enjoy the present.

When I look back on my life's journey, I feel fortunate. All the good times and bad times have been wonderful opportunities. I've been blessed by the people who surround me, who teach me, as my grandmother did, about the process of living. Some lessons are new, and others are taught by those you least suspect...like three nieces.

Lindsey is a free spirit teenager who truly embraces the present and loves who she is now. She lives each day to the fullest. A critical thinker who questions those aspects of our world she doesn't understand, Lindsey is filled with more knowledge about history, music, and world issues than most adults. Callie, on the other hand, has taught me if I speak, sing or love from the inside out, there is nothing I cannot do. She has the most compassionate heart of anyone I have ever met. There is no challenge I cannot meet. And, Emily has taught me that life should be fun. This funny and intelligent seven year old knows what she wants, dances like no one is watching, and sings so all can hear. She paints pictures on canvas with her words.

Here are a few other lessons on living life's journey I've picked up on the way:

• Don't be afraid to stretch your abilities and talents—you might surprise yourself.

- Don't second-guess yourself or your decisions—you will always live in "what ifs." Once you make a decision, embrace it.

- Surround yourself with others who are dreamers—others who see beyond where they are. They see where they can be.

- Find mentors, people you look to for support. People who challenge you. They will keep you motivated and hold you accountable. They will make sure you do what you said you would do.

- Never stop being a student! We'll never learn all that this world has to offer.

- Know that you are going to make mistakes—if you don't take risks, you will never know what the possibilities could have been.

- Learn to enjoy quiet time.

- Make a list of all of the things that you want to accomplish—where you want to travel, what people see in you, who you want to be to others and to yourself, and what you want to do in this life! You only get one chance. It's your life. LIVE IT!

- Dream BIG!

Dr. Mari Ann Callais

Love and Compassion

A SHAMROCK IN MY LIFE

You bring a twinkle to my eye and a grin to my face.
Bending always toward the light, never clouded with fear,
lending an ear, speaking only good cheer.

A symbol of kindness, strength, and genuine warmth—with eyes
that shine with a radiant flow,
your four petals are as soft as your glow.

A spirit so gentle, wrapped in a giggle of laughter—all the world
delights in the treat of your goodness.

You, a good luck charm—you, a shamrock in my life!

Patti Geib Holmes

CONSIDERATION COUNTS

What can you do today to make someone else's day?
Be on time. Show up with enthusiasm instead of being shown up by others.

Say what you mean and mean what you say.

Don't be afraid to fail, and learn to fail gracefully.

Remember that image is nothing; action is everything. Open a door.

Live today like it's your last day on Earth, because one day you'll be right.

Look in people's eyes when they talk.

Surround yourself with people who make your life worthwhile.

Pick up after yourself. Leave the world cleaner than you found it.

Speak kindly, and with integrity.

Demonstrate to everyone you meet that you are a person of great character.

Be a friend to yourself; enjoy time alone.

You are the only person you're guaranteed to spend the rest of your life with.

Buy a coffee for someone standing behind you in line.

Be aware of the people around you. Take care not to impose on or inconvenience those around you; as you wouldn't like them to impose on you.

Thank someone who never gets thanked.

Understand that you don't have to see good things in everyone; just try to believe that everyone is capable of good. Ask, "How can I help?"

Share joy. Every day, tell someone what's really great about them.

Let someone in line go ahead of you.

In a crowd, make the effort to say "hello" to people.

Write thank-you cards instead of e-mailing pixels of thanks. It will mean more.

Mean more.

Curtis Zimmerman

HOW BIG IS YOUR BUCKET?

"Too often we visit the well of divine abundance with
a teacup instead of a bucket."

- Elinor MacDonald

Imagine you are walking alone through a beautiful forest. It is a perfect day with blue sky and white, fluffy summer clouds. The sun shines through the leaves and you hear birds, an occasional squirrel, and your feet trotting on the soft pine needles. The solitude is a welcome contrast to the busy days and nights at work, your family, friends and other demands in your life.

As you realize how thirsty you are, you come upon a natural, bottomless spring with the cleanest, clearest, coldest water you have ever seen. You cup your hands and dip them into the stream. Refreshed by the drink and the serenity of the woods, you head toward home reminding yourself to bring a cup on your next visit. As an added reminder you write "bring cup on walk" on your to-do list and put a picture of a cup on your bulletin board.

The next day, you walk out to the spring and this time you take a cup. For weeks, you make this a daily ritual. Grateful for the endless supply of not just water, but of peace, confidence, clarity, freedom and motivation you feel when you drink from the spring. One day you realize you have been limiting yourself to one small cup of water when, in fact, this never-ending resource could provide you with so much more—maybe a bucket next time?

You take your largest bucket on your next walk excited about how your peace, confidence, clarity, freedom and motivation will increase by drinking more of the crystal spring water. You begin brainstorming ways to apply what you are learning to your entire life: your work, your fitness, and your other interests. You have never felt so creative, productive, focused and alive!

When you get to the spring, you fill your bucket and drink until you are "overflowing"—in fact, you quickly discover that there is no way you can possibly drink all the water. No matter how much you drink, you are sure there is always more than enough. You think, "If I could find a way to get the bucket of water home, I could share it with anyone who needs it."

You finish what you can, water a meadow with what's left, and RUN all the way home.   Seems the bucket idea was good in theory only.   Now what? You think: "Maybe I could fill a bucket and bring it back. Hmmm...too heavy. Maybe I could build an aqueduct. Too complicated. Maybe I could move into the woods and live next to the spring. No, too weird." In a moment of inspiration, you find the answer.

"I will tell my friends about the bottomless spring and the opportunity for feeling peaceful, confident, clear, free and motivated. We can go there together and take buckets. We will help each other carry the water back. They will tell their friends. Their friends will tell their friends. And because the spring is ever-giving, there will always be enough for everyone."

Before you go to bed, you make a list of people to tell about the spring. You sleep well knowing you have found a way to pass on what you have seen, felt and learned.

"This is too good to keep to myself!" you say as your head hits the pillow. Soon after, winding roads, blue skies, and open fields appear in your dreams. In the morning, you wake, ready to spread the joy and find more buckets.

How big is your bucket?

Kristin Skarie

OPEN YOUR HEART

There's no doubt about it. We long to belong. We want relationships that nurture our inner spirit. We want to live in communities that utilize our talents. We want to be the very best we can be. We want to love ourselves, and others.

As a nation, we value diversity, expression and freedom of speech. Yet still we close our hearts to others every day. People need people, it's true, but so many different people live on this planet. Human beings are as diverse as blades of grass on an immense and far-reaching field. No two of us are alike. But what can we do to build better relationships with other people, no matter who they are?

Commit, commit, commit. If you've ever been in a long term relationship, you know there are times when you want to give up. You may wonder if the emotional roller coaster of a relationship is really worth it. The more you get to know someone, the more obvious your differences become. Resist the urge to retreat when the going gets rough. Realize that a common bond brought you and your partner together.

Don't give up so quickly! Work through tough conversations. Face conflict. It's a good bet that you will learn more about your partner by addressing a conflict than ignoring it. Face those problems head on. Your relationship will improve as a result.

Admit you don't know everything. We are born different. It's okay not to know about people of another race, creed, nationality or sexual orientation. But don't let your fear prevent you from getting to know people who are different from you. We live in such a climate of political correctness. It scares most of us to be honest with others, if we suspect that we could be labeled as "racist" or "prejudiced." On the other hand, be careful about believing you know everything about diversity just because you have a black or Latino friend, have attended a religious experience different from your own, or saw *Brokeback Mountain* two times. We are born different, and it takes a long time to get to know all those who are different from you. Accept what you might not know. You may find yourself in a relationship with someone vastly different from you—and those are often the best relationships!

Do better. You probably get up every morning trying to do your best. You begin your day hoping to brighten someone's life. You wake up with good intentions. But you know what? You can do better. We all can. Without realizing it, we hurt other people from time to time. Realize your limitations, but strive to overcome them. Be conscious of others. Know that each day brings an opportunity to improve somebody's world. That's a great power—and a great responsibility. Don't take it lightly!

Crave knowledge. Have you ever heard the saying: "Just because you are doesn't mean you understand?" How about: "Just because you're not, doesn't mean you can't?" If you've ever been the only (fill in the blank) in the room, you know this position comes with the burden of representing an entire population. People assume you speak for everyone in that particular group, even though you can't hope to know what everyone is thinking. Speak from experience, but realize that you don't have all the answers. No one person can speak for an entire race, nationality, or sexual orientation.

Even if you don't have a lot in common with someone, you can still open your heart to them. Look at it as an opportunity to learn. Listen. Don't judge. Be an ally.

Let your heart grow wings. We don't treat everyone equally. There's injustice in this world, it's true. Recognize the signs of oppression, when other groups of people find their freedoms suppressed, their voices silenced. In such cases, one open heart can make a difference.

How can you right the wrongs in the world, when on the surface, they seem insurmountable? Grow wings. Risk speaking up. Advocate change. You'd be surprised what a difference one voice can make.

Listen up. Do you talk over other people? Are you jumping to the end of a sentence before your partner finishes it? Slow down. You will never be understood if you don't take the time to understand others. Sometimes we are so busy trying to be heard that we're not hearing.

In your next conversation, focus on what the other person is saying and doing. Listen carefully to non-verbal communication. Respond to what isn't being said, but read. Enjoy the silence.

Face your discomfort. Few people enjoy conflict. But you can't live in a diverse community if you aren't willing to step outside of your comfort zone. Don't avoid discomfort when you have a chance to face it— and eliminate it!

Break down your hidden fears. Overcome your insecurities. Defeat your prejudices and stereotypes. They're only holding you back from intimacy and love. Surviving difficult relationships, enduring hard conversations, and rising above turmoil will make you stronger.

You'll begin building bridges.

Heal thyself. Everyone's been hurt at some point. Maybe opening up to someone, or trusting someone, has left you broken. You took a risk and lost. Maybe your pain was caused by a particular person or group during your childhood, and as an adult you don't want to relive that agony. These are valid feelings. They are your feelings.

As a pastor, I believe in the power of forgiveness as a tool for letting go of pain. Forgiveness often starts by forgiving yourself first—otherwise, you won't be able to forgive others. Where there is no forgiveness, there is no love—or worse yet, there is indifference.

Take your time. Opening your heart is a life-long process. It took you a lifetime to acquire your attitudes, desires, and beliefs.

There are no quick fixes.

Give yourself the time you need to identify what holds you back from being part of diverse relationships and communities. Own your ignorance. Make an effort to unlearn the behaviors that you are least proud of—the ones holding you back form healthy relationships.

Acknowledge, celebrate and appreciate (you deserve it.) Do you know people who see the glass half empty? They operate from a deficit model, only seeing the negative. You may not be perfect. As a civilized society, we still have much work to do. But if we only see the problems and don't acknowledge our personal and collective progress, we are likely to create a culture of hopelessness. At the same time, we dishonor our efforts to love one another, including the efforts of those who came before us. There is hope!

People improve. Society changes. Hearts will open. I've watched it happen before my very eyes. Individuals, however, often change much faster than communities. The challenge with culture change is that it's a slow process. Many of those who try to change a culture for the better lose hope. I choose not to join them.

People have an incredible capacity to love. We have the tenacity and skill to overcome prejudice and explore ways to build our communities. We can choose to open our hearts to diversity.

Young people give me hope. I see heterosexuals, Christians, men, and able-bodied folks who are working to change cultures, to make life better for themselves and those around them. I see people of color, people with different sexual orientations, and people of all faiths, all finding their voices. They are all empowered. They are all agents of change.

Their hearts are open. Is yours?

Dr. Jamie Washington

SUPER HEROES
AND HEROINES

*"Gandhi was an ordinary man who invented an
extraordinary possibility for humanity and lived his
commitment to that possibility with integrity."*

- Landmark Education

Never doubt that you are a super hero or heroine! We often
make the mistake of idealizing our heroes and heroines in
ways that make them different from other average human beings.
Each of us is capable of heroism, if only we realize the potential
within us and how to access our deepest humanity. Are you willing to do what it takes to discover the hero within? Do you have
a fight in you?

Consider what it takes to become the best person you can be
(to be fully actualized and connected to a deep sense of humanity)—to realize your heroism!

- You can take risks and make mistakes because you have good
  intentions, and know the value of mistakes is that you learn
  from them;

- You face terrific challenges with courage and grace because you
  know you have true power within you, and can use that power
  to make a difference;

- You are confident that your life is meaningful. You know your purpose;

- You live free of denial and hopelessness—you give yourself permission to live in passion and joy!

Being super takes work. Some days are easier than others. The trick is to give the best of who you are always—and forgive yourself when you fall short. When you reach for your outer most limits the possibilities are endless. Being super also takes an enhanced understanding of how our approach to the world impacts our future.

Unfortunately, many people view the world from a win-lose scenario. The "haves" are the clear winners over the "have nots." Understandably, people who experience a lack of resources, opportunities and fair treatment are viewed more as "losers" in this artificial game; yet people with ample resources, access and respectful treatment are also the "losers" because their lifestyle and conditioning has forced them to abandon parts of their humanity! In truth, they are disconnected from an immense passion to end suffering and injustice. They are the "losers" because they have lost sight of their incredible personal power to end inequality in the world.

Looking at the world from a win-lose perspective gives privilege to some while restricting access to others. Our system of privilege pits people against each other in a battle for superficial things that don't bring happiness only mistrust; teaches judgments instead of compassion; creates fear instead of courage; fuels competition instead of collaboration; disconnects us from our loving power; perpetuates polarization and encourages denial, guilt and blame instead of encouraging our individual and collective responsibility for change.

Reclaiming our super powers (i.e. deepest sense of humanity) and helping others become super heroes and heroines is ultimately a commitment to ourselves—who we are as human beings and who we are willing to become. In this pursuit, we get our best selves back and create a space for others to become their best selves. Compassion replaces self-interest as we learn to overcome our conditioning and rise to our greatness where all have access to lives of dignity, freedom and purpose. There would be no "winners" or "losers."

To have super powers doesn't mean you need to take a vow of poverty; rather, you need to increase your capacity for love, courage and compassion. Surrender to be the best you can be. Believe in the human capacity to conquer the cultural malaise of our times; hopelessness, cynicism, and resignation. Make a decision to act courageously, compassionately and consistently to create the world we wish for the future.

Use your super powers to see through the walls that hold you back; to break the chains that bind you. Once you realize that you to are "super," then you'll be leaping tall buildings in no time.

Top Ten Ways to Be Super:

1. Be good to yourself by striving to maximize your effectiveness. Get exercise, nutrition, and plenty of rest. Allow yourself to heal...and yes...even super heroes "play" on occasion!

2. Feel good about yourselves and others. Be fully grounded so you can grow and avoid becoming defensive or judgmental of others. Deepen your compassion. Realize that you, too, can change the world in time.

3. Surrender the pursuit of the superficial in the land of excess. Put down your remote and find out how you can help others. (Check out www.newdream.org to discover ways to take action!)

4. Surround yourself with people who care about you. Even Batman had a butler! To accomplish your goals, you must have friends and family who love you, listen, give advice, and take care of you when you most need help. Set up relationships and structures so you can thrive in your mission!

5. Reclaim your childlike zest for life! Remember when

you were young and nothing seemed impossible? Recapture that enthusiasm.

6. Forgive yourself and forgive others. Taking responsibility to make peace in your life—it will set you free.

7. Find courage and hope in all the good things around you. Don't be distracted by the sensationalistic spina-rama of mainstream media. Realize that there are good people, as well as, good things in this world—including you!

8. Appreciate, appreciate, appreciate yourself and others.

9. Know you have an extraordinary will to do the impossible. We are all blessed with countless gifts. It's our calling to share these with the world.

10. Never surrender your commitment to your own transformation. Share the joy and aliveness you experience as you reclaim your humanity to inspire and transform others. Open doors and invite others to join in your vision. Just when you think all hope is lost, remember one thing: You are an amazing human being with all of the super powers you need to create the world you wish for!

Marilyn Levin

WILLING HEART
HELPING HANDS

Leading up to Katrina were some of the worst hurricane seasons on record. It wasn't always the catastrophic punch of one hurricane which caused extensive damage, as much as it was a combination of punches hitting the same areas. Although not reaching the magnitude of Katrina's destruction and devastation, hurricanes hitting the southern eastern coast were devastating none the less. They changed many people's lives and caused significant damage to homes, animal habitats and the landscape.

Although wind speeds, amount of rain fall, and overall impact of hurricanes may vary greatly, the human capacity to show compassion and help those in need—including even the smallest of human creatures—is endless and knows no limitations. You can find different needs for love, hope and recovery—but when they all are met by 100% of someone's compassion, the human heart beats the hurricane every time!

Here is a story about strong winds, lots of rain and a little animal in need of rescue. It's also the story of a willing heart...

Tree limbs of all shapes and sizes and debris came whipping across my friend's yard. The hurricane sirens could be heard in the distance, and the sky was growing darker. When the eye of the storm finally passed, my friend knew she had a small window of time to let out her dog—a big German Shepherd in need of relieving himself.

As she glanced out the window to check on her dog, she noticed him wrestling with something in the rising pond next to her house. There was almost three feet of water rushing into the former ditch by now. In spite of her calls, the dog was relentlessly pursuing something caught in the rising water.

My friend hurried outside to investigate. When she got to the ditch, she saw a tiny creature struggling beneath the surface of the water. Realizing there was little time for decision making; she ran her dog into the house and went back to save it!

Waste deep with howling winds, my friend reached in for the flailing, frightened and exhausted animal. Unsure what it was—or if it was of the biting variety (like a rat) she weighed her options. I'm sure she also considering what she would do if it was a rat and it bit her! The longer she held back, the more hopeless the animal became.

It was now submerged for four seconds at a time and had stopped swimming. As it began to go under for what was probably the last time, my friend's heart instructed her to act. She stuck both arms under the surface and felt something grab her sleeve, clutching her arm as it made it's way out of the water. It was a baby squirrel.

The baby squirrel climbed the length of her arm and rested next to her neck. It was in shock, panting and shivering. The tiny lungs sounded as if they would collapse.

Careful not to touch the squirrel with her bare hands, my friend delicately carried her victim to warm shelter inside the house. By the time they reached the kitchen, the baby squirrel was sound asleep, breathing with effort. My friend was saddened by the possibility her efforts had been in vain, but continued on her quest to save one of God's creatures.

With the storm at full speed and her dog trying to watch through the peep whole of the adjoining bedroom, my friend made her guest a nest in an old shoebox, and placed a fig in it. She then watched the little squirrel sleep.

After an hour there came a rustling sound. When she opened the lid, the squirrel stood on its hind legs, fig in both hands and a look of victory in its eyes. My friend sprung into action. The wind was picking up again so she knew she didn't have much time to reunite the baby squirrel with its mother. Nonetheless, she decided she had to try.

Putting the animal's welfare ahead of her own, my friend carried the shoebox outside and put it by the tree next to the ditch turned pond. Then a miracle happened. The likely mother squirrel raced to her child, stood on her hind legs, and let the wandering infant have it in squirrel language! More specifically, "mama" squirrel language! As soon as the tiny squirrel heard the clicking noise and looked out of the shoebox, you could almost hear a *Disney* music score. The two animals bounded towards each other, frolicked and hugged—just like humans!

What followed brought great comfort to my friend and renewed her trust in the natural instinct to do whatever it takes to help a living thing. She watched from her porch as the mother squirrel attempted to get her baby back up the tree. The baby was clearly too tired and had no intention of following her mother up the trunk—despite the mothers numerous trips to her baby and back up the log like a game of Follow the Leader. The tiny creature wasn't playing.

The sky began to get dark again and the more experienced squirrel could sense danger. My friend sensed it as well, and began to take steps back into the wind and rain to protect the tiny squirrel for a second time. Suddenly, the mama squirrel sprinted over to her baby, picked it up by the scruff of its neck, and carried it up the log to safety.

Happy Endings. Two months later, my friend reported seeing the same mother and baby squirrel running across her yard. This obviously brought her great joy and a humbled sense of satisfaction in knowing her role in the story. She knew the pair's lively demonstration was a sign of their appreciation and a way of saying "thank you." During one frolic across her yard, the smaller squirrel actually stopped and looked directly at my friend. She knew it was his way of saying, "Thank you. I made it."

What would you have done in a similar situation? With a hurricane on the way, would you have taken the time and risked your own safety to come to the aid of another living thing? After all, this isn't really a story of a brave human being saving a tiny squirrel—it's a tale of the human heart and how a little compassion goes a long way.

Whether you are offering a smile to a sad child, taking a plate of food to a shut in, holding a door open for someone whose hands can't grip the way they once did, or even helping a tiny animal climb to the safety; the small acts of kindness can make the biggest differences in the world. Helping someone (or something) in need isn't all that hard—it's often as simple as having a willing heart and helping hands.

Elaine Penn

WHAT IF YOU...

"We won't believe that the world can change
until we experience ourselves changing.
Hope is not what we find in evidence; it
is what we become in action".

- Frances Moore Lappe

What if you...
Cheer when anyone scores a goal; Treasure and celebrate people as if they had only had a short time to live; Evaluate people by their kindness, generosity and altruism instead of their income, status and power; Stop buying unnecessary things for people we care about and use that money to work toward the world they wish for in their dreams for humanity?

What if you. . .

Work to heal the polarization that is tearing us apart and join with our adversaries to serve a mutual cause; Praise your adversaries and enemies for the good they do in the world instead of just cursing them for the damage they do?

What if you. . .

Decided not to let your past influence your future regardless of the conditioning you've received; Rise to the occasion; Appreciate challenging situations; Remain free of judgment; Use the very best of who you are to inspire the best in others?

What if you. . .

Transform the ways in which you fulfill your need to compete, excel, and test your limits; Dig deeper inside yourself and see what you are made of; Use your passion, drive and pursuit of excellence to create a peaceful and sustainable planet; Confront your fears and move beyond your current limitations to end hunger, and violence; Create environments where people feel cared for, supported and challenged in healthy ways?

What if you. . .

Channel your bountiful resources to improve the world in some way?

What if you...

Inspired possibility and hope in others?

Marilyn Levin

Relationships

GREAT RELATIONSHIPS

Have you met that special someone? The person you enjoy being around and want to date? Are you already in a fulfilling dating relationship, or are you still looking? Do you get along well with your family members and friends?

These are rather tough questions which come with rather easy answers: "yes" or "no." You might not like your answers, but they are your answers—your truth. If you want to be in a great relationship, you have to work for it. You have to get involved and accept another truth: You deserve happiness in your relationships—including friendships, family relations, office exchanges, and yes... intimate dating relationships!

No more settling for or tolerating those individuals who make up your world. You deserve to experience joy, honor, fulfillment and happiness from those around you. No more lowering your standards, or accepting that your relationship with someone "is what it is." Get involved in your relationships and watch them improve!

Steps to Great Relationships. Understand your past. Understanding your past greatly helps you create a positive future. When it comes to dating, for example, most people fall into a cycle of repeating the same behaviors and choices which have only brought them back to where they began—alone. Have you ever said, "I constantly find myself going after someone who is wrong for me?" or "Why don't my friends appreciate me?"

To get to a greater understanding, consider the value in writing down related questions. Using the examples above, write down questions like "Why would I be afraid to be with someone who is actually right for me?" or "What is it about my friends that I appreciate?" Writing is a wonderful tool for examining your role in relationships, identifying mistakes before they happen, and challenging yourself to change behaviors that sabotage great relationships.

Another way to use writing as a tool for great relationships is to make a list of your relationship goals. Be specific. What exactly do you expect from the ideal partner, companion, friend, colleague, or sibling? (Note that I didn't say "perfect" in the previous description because that's an unrealistic standard. Are you perfect?) What will you need to do to make this relationship work? How do you want to be treated? What are you willing to give? Be honest. Start your answers with phrases like, "I need..." or "I want to feel..." or "I am willing to..."

It's difficult to be truthful about your own role in establishing and maintaining great relationships, especially when it comes to identifying your strengths and weaknesses. Your best relationships might just be with those who compliment your strengths and weaknesses, as opposed to those who are just like you!

Create standards. When reflecting upon your desired outcomes for a particular relationship, ask yourself if your standards are too high or too low. For instance, seek the friendships that make you a better person and allow you to maintain your values, morals and self-respect. Your relationships should build you up, not make you feel inferior, inadequate or unimportant.

Try writing down a list of what matters to you. Write down all of your standards on punctuality, courtesy, kindness, respect, honor, communication, honesty, etc. Next to each standard, give yourself a score ranging from one (lowest) to ten (highest,) based upon how well you perform or reach each standard in your relationships. Is there consistency between how you want to be treated and how you treat others? Are you in relationships based upon lower standards of acceptance, and if so, why?

Another strategy for creating relationship standards is to discover (or own) the standards you do bring to your relationships by asking those who make up the other half of those relationships. Sound scary? Don't be nervous; your friends, siblings, and colleagues often value things about you which you might not see as an asset! Ask people to write down things about you that make you unique, special and valuable. You can do the same for them. Then, compare each other's lists. Discuss your relationships. You will realize that others see strengths in you that you don't notice. Your list of standards just grew!

Cherish this list. Read your list out loud when you wake up each morning. No one else has to hear how you want to be treated and how you need to treat others. There's no denying that you desire in others that which you seek for yourself. Honor these values. See if you agree with the following sample list of personal standards:

- ❏ I have compassion for others.
- ❏ I respect all people.
- ❏ My body is precious.
- ❏ I do the right thing.
- ❏ Honesty is a sign of self-respect.
- ❏ I am trustworthy.
- ❏ Keeping confidences shows character.
- ❏ I am considerate.
- ❏ I like to be complimented.

At the end of the day, ask yourself whether or not your actions and decisions fit your list of standards or not. Consider whether your list is complete or if there are other standards you can add.

When you can identify what matters to you in your exchanges, you are less likely to hurt others or make them feel unworthy. You are more likely to seek relationships where your values will be honored, not compromised. You are more likely to speak freely and share your honest opinions about life. You will also be more capable of discussing these standards as part of maintaining a healthy and fulfilling relationship.

Ask first. The healthiest relationships are built on self-respect and respect for others. This is most often accomplished by communicating openly and honestly. That's easy to say and hard to carry out. Communication for great relationships requires practice. You must believe that if you can't talk with respect toward the other person in your relationship, then you need to either change your communication patterns, or stop talking and end the relationship.

How do you demonstrate respect in your actions and decisions? Here's an example based on a dating relationship: Picture yourself sitting in an intimate location with your partner, holding hands and looking into each other's eyes. You lean in, smile and ask before acting, "May I kiss you?" This behavior demonstrates a lack of assumption on your part, and shows respect for the other person's personal space. Giving your partner a choice before you do something is always the right choice to make.

The same principle holds true for friendships. Picture yourself standing in front of the movie theatre with a friend. It's been a long week for both of you, and a particularly tough week for your friend. Instead of your usual habit of paying for your own tickets, you look at your friend and say, "This one's on me. What would you like to see?" Giving your friend the choice in what movie you will see shows him or her you feel badly about the bad week.

Having great relationships takes work and self-examination. You need to be honest with yourself about the things you bring to your relationships, and what is attractive about you! Enjoy your relationships and take pleasure in knowing that someone is giving time to be around you. Great relationships are made up of great people!

Mike Domitrz

MOMENT OF TRUTH

When I was in college, I had a beautiful girlfriend named Michelle. She had a great sense of humor, came from a wonderful family, and was very intelligent. The best thing about Michelle? She really loved me.

Being loved as Michelle loved me was new. Throughout the awkward years of high school, girls didn't even like me. I knew rejection and I knew it well. Now, I was loved. What more could a guy want? This was the girl of my dreams. It felt really good.

If it felt so good, why did I know it was really so wrong? We were having so much fun, spending lots of time together, and I wasn't alone anymore. My heart was shared. But there was something wrong and I had to face it. When you went beneath the exterior, we weren't compatible. We simply didn't share some important values—the values relationships require to last. We kept on dating.

Part of my self discovery included getting to know me better. What did I want? What was important? How could I live my faith? What type of person will make me happy? I was also learning the very difficult lesson—a rite of passage most college students encounter—the difference between infatuation and love. Was this really love? And, if it was love, why did I keep questioning it?

Before long, I found myself facing the "moment of truth." This is the point when you commit, one way or the other. Gray is replaced with black or white. You realize there are absolutes. You honor yourself, your moral convictions, values and faith by making a decision to act. This is when you decide to let your actions support your beliefs.

My "moment of truth" came while having an important conversation with myself. Do you ever have those? You ask questions out loud and hope you will miraculously answer them. My conversation began, "Do I break up with this wonderful (yet not perfect for me) woman? Do I let go of someone who loves me?" I continued my internal talk when the phone rang. Michelle was inviting me over. Her roommate had gone home for the weekend and she had the room to herself. I knew what she was saying, and what she wanted. I also knew I had a decision to make.

Unable to face my "moment of truth" at that particular moment, I got dressed and started walking over to her room. I said out loud, "Don't do this. You know this is wrong. You're going to regret this." As I approached the building, my pace slowed. I got closer to the front door and stopped. In the glass I saw my reflection. Looking myself in the face, I said, "Who am I? What am I doing? What do I want?" I took my hand off of the doorbell and returned to my own room.

I broke up with Michelle. Not an easy thing for me to do. Instead of getting support, my friends said, "Yo! What kind of guy breaks up with such a gorgeous girl?" It wasn't easy for me to hurt someone's feelings. Not to mention, this good old boy was about to be alone again. But I was ready to be truthful and do the right thing. It was time to grow into my faith, not away from it.

The weeks and months to follow were some of the saddest of my life, but not for obvious reasons. My relationship with Michelle took a path neither one of us could have imagined.

Not long after our breakup, Michelle was asked to have a test to rule out HIV. She needed my support and I agreed to go to the doctor's office with her. "How could this happen?" she screamed after learning that her test was positive. Looking at this beautiful woman, I thought, "This is unbelievable. This kind of stuff doesn't happen to someone like Michelle." I now understand all too well that sexually-transmitted diseases don't discriminate.

Michelle later explained that she contracted the disease from her first and only sexual partner before college—a guy she dated back in high school who had told her she was his first, as well. Apparently, he wasn't being honest with her.

Eighteen months later, Michelle died. My sense of loss was great. We had become so close and had found our common ground. I visited her in the hospital, tried to keep her optimistic, and tried to be a true friend. The shock of her loss is still so real.

Why did this happen? Why can't people be honest with one another? Why is it so hard to make the right decisions when they need to be made—at the right time? When you find yourself facing your "moment of truth," consider looking at your face. Stand in front of your reflection and ask yourself, *"Who am I? What am I doing? What do I want?"* Care enough about your present, and your future. Don't act until you hear the answers.

Lance Smith

SECOND CHANCES

*"I'd rather have five minutes of something great,
than a lifetime of nothing special."*

- *Cindy Brock*

Ever wonder what your relationships (and life) would be like
now if you could turn back time and get another try—a second chance? Armed with all the invaluable lessons learned from
your misspoken words, misinterpreted perceptions and mistakes,
imagine how much greater the odds of making your relationships
more meaningful, lasting and mutually enjoyable—if you got a "do
over" or chance to try again.

Unfortunately, life is not a dress rehearsal...you can't turn back
the clock and hope the person you still long to be with will come
down with a case of selective amnesia so you could meet him or
her all over again "for the first time!" The best you—or any of
us—can do is to learn from our previous friendships, relationships
and dating experiences. Instead of focusing on the hurt, pain, or
the joy, consider why you came to feel those emotions in the first
place. What was it about how you thought, spoke and behaved
in those relationships which might be helpful information to you
now? Within the pages of your past are the rules of engagement for
your future relationships.

I've put together a list of the many lessons I've learned over the
past two decades speaking and writing on dating and relationships—

in no particular order—which serve as important insights into what human beings seek out of their interactions with others. Whether a romantic involvement, casual acquaintance or lasting friendship, you can improve the quality of your relationships when you better understand and accept the realities (or rules) presented here:

- When people show you their true selves, believe them!

- The difference between hearing and listening is comprehension.

- People need to claim and appreciate their limitations, but not accept them as permanent.

- When we become fearful and inhibited, we stop living a full life.

- Anger is simply a blocked goal.

- Never attack another person's character.

- You can apologize, but you can never take back something you have said in anger.

- You never get back a wasted day.

- No desire is so strong that it justifies throwing away God's will to satisfy it.

- Gossip destroys the life of the soul.

- Successful relationships don't begin by finding the right person; they begin by being the right person.

- You cannot live a lie, as others will see through you like glass.

- If you look clearly enough, a person will tell you everything about themselves the instant they approach you and before they ever say a word.

- The person who is the least invested has all the control in a relationship.

- Critical moments in our life are snapshots that are frozen in time as pictures in our heart.

- Conflicts become more intense as the stakes become higher.

- You view the world from the pictures in your heart.

- At times you need to spring clean your soul and rearrange your mental closet.

- Forgiveness is giving up the right to hurt someone who has previously hurt you.

- Men measure their self-worth and value by what they do and what they are good at.

- Women measure their self-worth and value by who they are.

- It is impossible to consistently act in a way that is inconsistent with the way you view yourself.

- We rarely spend time in solitude because we don't know enough about the person we will be spending time with!

- Rejection is like a bridge—you'll get over it!

- There is a fine line between serendipity and stalking.

- When in doubt, err in the direction of romance!

- We take with us a piece of every person with whom we interact.

- A light is only noticed when it is too dim, too bright, flickering or burned out.

- What matters most is how you see yourself.

- If you fight hard enough for your limitations, they will become yours.

David Coleman

SUCCESSFUL DATING

D o you wish dating wasn't so hard—or hurtful? Below is a list of ten helpful tips for having dates based upon mutual respect, fun and possibility.

No dating games. You constantly hear people talking about being in the "dating game," yet they fail to realize that games pit people against each other. There is a winner and a loser. Healthy dating requires a mutual success story. Therefore, eliminate all games, tactics and strategies. Simply go out and get to know your date better.

Plan sunlight dates. Go out during the day—something new and different! Go on a picnic. Go bowling. Pick an activity that will most likely encourage laughter. It's much easier to be yourself in the day, than having to be this incredibly "romantic" individual in the evening. Afternoon dating also takes away the pressure of instant intimacy.

No pity for you. Only date people you truly want to date and can trust. Accepting a date because you feel "sorry" for someone is disrespectful and uncaring because it raises hopes and is misleading. To turn down a date, say, "Thank you for asking. I believe in being honest and don't feel a connection between us. However, I am honored that you asked."

Stick to the standards. Before you go on a date with someone new, write down your "dating standards." For example, you might include on your list: I don't want to be kissed unless I am asked. Unfortunately, many people make the mistake of lowering their standards in order to "win" over their date. If you are going to lose someone because you are determined to maintain high personal standards, then lose that person! You deserve to be with someone who respects you for being you. Whether the date is going badly or well, stick to your standards.

Only listen to you. Friends love to tell friends what to do. Sometimes, they encourage risky and dangerous behaviors, or brag about things they really haven't done in an effort to make themselves sound better. Above all, listen to your instincts.

Ask first and answer honestly. Before you even think about becoming intimate on a date, ask if your partner agrees. If your partner asks for intimacy, be honest. You never owe your partner anything you don't want to share, especially something as precious and sacred as intimate acts of love. If you are asked, but are not comfortable, say, "That is so cool that you asked, but no. This is not what I want right now." Be clear.

Remember it takes two to tango. Dating is a partnership based upon mutual respect. Regardless of how different your date's beliefs might be from yours, remember that he or she is a person. Avoid criticizing, interrupting and dismissing the other person. Hear them out. Talk about your differences. Learn from the exchange. You may just be misunderstanding each other. If you clearly understand your differences and aren't interested in the other person, make it a respectful last date!

Don't alter your judgment. Avoid alcohol and drugs—especially on dates! Any substance that can impair your judgment and decision making can be extremely dangerous. If your partner is trying to pressure you into drinking, take notice! This pressure should be a warning sign of possible disrespect, carelessness and trouble. You should end this date early!

Listen, listen, listen. Be careful about disclosing your entire life history, including previous relationship failures. Ask open ended questions designed to get to know the other person. For example, "Tell me about your greatest travel adventure," and then listen attentively. Don't interrupt or start sharing your greatest travel adventure! Everyone likes to be heard.

Talk, talk, talk. As you plan a date, involve your partner. Give a few of your ideas and then ask which is most appealing to him or her. By discussing how you will be spending your time together early on, you demonstrate the significance you place on equality in a relationship.

Dating should be fun and leave you feeling better about yourself—not worse. Start putting into practice one or all of the above ten tips for successful dating and you may find yourself meeting wonderful people and having great fun in your new relationships!

Mike Domitrz

THE VALENTINES IN YOUR LIFE

Who are the Valentines in your life? Were they...
    Smart...funny...mixed-up?
Clean-cut...calm...challenging...full of integrity...so tender...hard-
    working?
Handsome...hurtful...faithful...mean...gentle...mind-boggling?
Humble...anxious...modest...polite?
Self-centered...curt...engaging...inconsiderate...crazy...gracious...
    just like your Dad?
Forgiving...debonair...insincere...warm...good to your kids...
    puzzling...sexy?
Witty...a great cook...boring...suave?
Well-read...ignorant...a true friend...beautiful?
Insecure...adventurous...hilarious...striking...risky...wonderful...
    confusing...lovely?
Radiant...a replica of your mom...charming...clueless...sensitive...
    enchanting?
Conceited...brilliant...gorgeous...kindhearted?
Detached...healthy...elegant...vain...dazzling...a character...or a
    true delight?
Sometimes we listened.
Sometimes love was blind.
But each time we loved we learned.
And each time we gave up our heart we took a chance;

We learned how to be loved and how to love with deeper insight and care.

Patti Geib Holmes

TRUE FRIENDS

True friends are rare.
  Time spent with them is effortless.
Nobody keeps score.

There is no jealousy.
Gossip is non-existent.
You have each other's best interests at heart.

True friends are rare.
You hearts beat together in friendship.
Caring about each other is so easy.

David Coleman

Success

ACCELERATE YOUR DESTINY

"Preparation is the greatest invitation to the right opportunities!"

Destiny acceleration is the right of every great person, and since you are a person of greatness, this right is now yours as well. You possess the power to speed up or slow down your greatness. You can create your own destiny, success, abundance, prosperity, fulfillment, wealth, health, joy, peace, and miracle mentality. Open up your heart, mind and spirit to these powerful strategies. Live them daily.

Discover your purpose early in life! People sometimes end up doing a good job at the wrong things in life. They make decisions about their businesses, relationships and finances, for instance, which aren't consistent with what truly matters to them— their purpose. You must know your purpose, and you must be crystal clear about the ways you share your gifts.

Take the time to search your soul, inventory your gifts, talents, and passions. *What brings you happiness and fills your spirit? What do you want? Why do you want these things? How do you want them?* These are questions about and indicators of your purpose. When you have clarity of purpose, you are free to focus and accelerate your destiny. Without clarity, you risk going through life experimenting, testing, and constantly searching for what is already inside of you. Listen to what brings you joy.

Another method for discovering your purpose is to consider what it is you don't like about the way you spend your time. Make a list. When something is always a struggle, it may be time to recognize that there's a reason...it's inconsistent with your purpose.

Commit to never being satisfied with your potential. Potential is nothing more than the gap that exists between where you are, and where you want to be. Most people are just like icebergs, 70-90% of their greatness remains hidden below the water line. Few make a deliberate decision to turn over the iceberg and maximize their greatness.

Do you have potential for more? Do you have the potential to do more, achieve more, give more, love more, contribute more, celebrate more, reward more, smile more, earn more, grow more, encourage more, save more, learn more, teach more, experience more, and just be more?

"Healthy dissatisfaction with your present is the birthplace for a great future!" - Dr. Mike Murdock

Create and seize destiny opportunities. Opportunity is defined as: "a set of circumstances creating a chance or possibility for advancement." One of the key differences between achieving our destiny and not achieving it is the ability to recognize, create, and maximize the opportunities which exist around us.

"The greatest opportunities in life are often disguised as hard work!" - Author Unknown

To move from the "normal ninety" into the "talented tenth" requires you to seek out, or proactively create (then maximize) your opportunities. Create opportunities for others along the way.

Consider why millions of people line up for days and days to get on American Idol, or get up each morning and go to work, or visit online dating websites—opportunity. They are actively creating circumstances that will allow them to experience new challenges and creative outlets. They are looking for ways to give to the world and discover new things about themselves.

"Opportunity always takes NOW for an answer!" - John Maxwell

Master and market your passion. Stop fast-forwarding and rewinding your life. Let it powerfully play out in your favor!

Tiger Woods would not be fulfilling his destiny if he just

"found" golf and let it go at that. Golf became his obsession. Don't be afraid of being obsessed by the pursuit of what matters to you. Jump in with both feet and master your passions, then have the confidence to share your talents, ideas and gifts with the world.

What is the one gift, talent, ability or skill you are willing to master in life? Who needs to know when you have mastered your gift? The most talented people in this world don't always get the most recognition; rather, it's the ones who know how to put their gifts out there for the benefit of others. Put your passion on display.

Write, talk about, and work your goals. Decide today to commit your goals, progress and destiny to paper. Dr. Mike Murdock notes, "A short pencil beats a long memory any day of the week!" Great inventions and business ideas begin as urgent thoughts scribbled on napkins and place mats. When you have moments of inspiration, quickly get your vision out of your head and onto paper. It's much easier to pursue what you can see.

Why not take the process a step further by creating a "vision wall" in your house? Create a wall full of pictures representing all the things you want to do, become and achieve. Look at it daily.

One of the most effective ways to turn your ideas, dreams and visions into destiny is to literally talk about them with others who are in a position to help you achieve them. You never know who knows someone, or who has an idea or contact to get you on your way. Share with those constructive people in your life, not with those who are "toxic," seeking only to hold you back and keep you down. I have learned to share my goals only with a very small, select group who can hold me accountable and are proud of my success.

"The reason I am more successful than most is because I have failed more than most!" - Robert Kyosaki

Overcome and capitalize on your pain. Pain is the greatest detour to greatness. Many people never realize their destiny in their careers, relationships, or spiritual lives because they quit out of pain. The litmus test of whether or not you can handle this thing called destiny is your ability to overcome the painful experiences and either let them go, or use them to your advantage. Pain will cause you to either get better, or get bitter!

There can be no success without some degree of failure and pain. One of my favorite authors, Dr. John C. Maxwell, encourages his readers to get "inspirationally dissatisfied" enough with their situation to make a radical shift into a positive and productive direction. This shift has the power to create success and move you from despair to your destiny.

My life is a testament to the value of bouncing back from pain faster than other people do. This can happen when you don't take painful situations personally. Pain (whether it be professional, personal, spiritual, emotional, or financial) is trying to tell you something is not right. In fact, it's quite wrong. What about your perspective, expectations, behavior, level of connectedness, attitude, ideology, habits, and so forth, needs inspection?

"If life knocks you down, that's not your fault. But if I come back a week later and you are still on the ground...that's your fault!" - Rev. Al Sharpton

Master the power of mentorship. A "mentor" is defined as a wise and trusted counselor or teacher. There is no age cap on mentors. There is no gender, racial or cultural cap either. You can be mentored by someone younger, older, a different color or nationality from you. It really does not matter. You are looking for someone to give you wise and trusted counsel and instruction.

Seek a mentor who can help you improve the areas in your life where you feel you need the most help. Mentors should be individuals you admire. You should respect their accomplishments, morals and ethics. They should be individuals with a giving spirit and commitment to your personal growth and the achievement of your destiny. Usually, those who have "been there and done that" serve as wonderful mentors.

Mentorship is a systematic investment in the people, paradigms, and principles that collapse time and empower rapid, sustained growth. They help you master your destiny! Who do you admire and respect for their accomplishments?

Better your best! People who achieve their destiny wake up every morning with the desire to do something that day to top what they did the day before. Maybe it's a commitment to learning something new, or meeting someone new. Maybe they dedicate themselves to noticing something they missed in nature yesterday, or expressing their gratitude for a blessing.

Input determines output, and if you put low quality things into your mind, you will get low quality things out. If you put great things in, of course great things will come back out. When life gets stale and boring, you must make a commitment to bringing about a fresh approach to that area each day.

Ways to keep it fresh include: reading one book per month, rather than one book per year, watching only one to two hours of television per day, or turning it off completely for a month.

How can you top yourself today? How can you be a better husband tomorrow than you were today? How can you be a more loving parent tomorrow than you were today? How can you show more integrity today than you did yesterday?

When asked which performance out of his hundreds of thousands was his best, James Brown replied, "The one I will do tomorrow!" How true. Your best is still inside you. Wake up tomorrow and better it!

"Empty the coins of your purse into your mind and your mind will fill your purse with coins." - Benjamin Franklin

Develop a winning personality. I will never forget the day that I met George Ross from the NBC hit television show *The Apprentice*. George Ross has been Donald Trump's Real Estate Attorney for more than twenty years! During our conversation, I asked him to share his top three strategies for success.

Despite having orchestrated over 700 different real estate transitions for The Donald, as well as being his close advisor, I was surprised when he smiled at me, put his hand on my shoulder, gave a gentle squeeze and said, "Son, you are gonna go very far in life, and you will be very successful in business!"

I smiled big and muttered, "Why? How do you know?"

The successful businessman across the table from me responded, "Because you ask awesome questions that empower you to inspire others, and that is a great trait to have. I picked up on it right away!" Then he continued to tell me the three great principles guiding his life and success. The first is to have a winning personality.

A "winning" personality is one which completes rather than competes, celebrates rather than complicates, and builds bridges rather than brick walls. A "winning" personality reflects how the totality of the whole is greater than the sum of its parts and becomes more empowered by empowering others to win. Families with winning personalities function like a team. They love each other, support each other, pray for each other, and invest in each other's passions.

Are you ready to achieve your destiny? The strategies above can get you there, if you commit to them. They will speed up your success—however you choose to define it. I hope part of your success is the desire to leave the world a better place because of your greatness.

Delatorro McNeal, II

FEAR OF SUCCESS

During my first semester as a graduate student, I took a course on the psychology of human motivation. One of my many semester assignments was to write a research paper analyzing and describing my personal view of any fears that had hindered me in the past, that I faced in the present, or were perceived as challenges in the future.

The core question of the assignment was: *What are the fears that hinder and block your success in life?* At the time, the only real fear I highlighted was a fear of failure (i.e. the fear of making mistakes and taking risks based on anticipated criticism or ridicule), or so I thought. Much to my dismay, after turning in my lengthy academic and scholarly research paper, I received the unfamiliar grade of a B-minus! Underneath my disappointing grade was the comment, "You have only written on the fear of failure—missing required content on the fear of success." That evaluation was provided by Dr. Carroll, my professor.

Immediately after class I asked him to explain his comments and the reasoning behind the grade. In his soft-spoken and mild-mannered way, he encouraged me to re-read the section in our textbook on the fear of success. I didn't want to do this and didn't! The only thing I wanted at that point in my life was an "A," and a better explanation from Dr. Carroll.

At the time, I did not understand his wisdom. I didn't care about growing personally and professionally based on an introspective writing and research assignment; I was grade-driven, 21 years old, young, stubborn, and grossly opinionated. I continued to protest but nothing changed as a result.

I did not fear success. Did my professor not recognize that I had made it to graduate school after almost failing out of my first semester at Elmhurst College? Growing up in the inner city of Chicago, I had beaten the odds for young black males between the ages of 18 and 25 by even making it to graduate school! Did he not acknowledge that I had successfully avoided the three P's—parole, prison, and probation? Dr. Carroll was out of his mind! Why would he even question a "success story" in the making?

I had graduated from high school in three years by the age of 17, and completed my BA in three-and-a-half years at 20. I intended to complete my first Master's degree in one-and-a-half years. I believed you couldn't do all this if you were really fearful of success! Despite my arguments, my graduate professor stood his ground. He encouraged me to re-read the chapter. I still refused; settling for what I felt was an undeserved grade of a B-minus.

After earning my graduate degree, I continued to read, research, and attend seminars on the subject of success. Through my studies, I noticed something very peculiar: the phrase "fear of success" kept resurfacing. The truth and wisdom which had eluded me earlier had suddenly become more apparent and relevant. Additionally, I was offered two professional opportunities of a life-time. The first was to teach full-time at Hennepin Technical College (Minnesota,) and the second was to teach part-time at the University of Minnesota.

At age 25, I had made it! I was finally in a place where I could quit all my meaningless jobs and focus on a teaching career in higher education. My dreams, prayers and passions were about to be realized.

Oddly enough, the more I contemplated my promising situation, the more I began to question my capabilities. Did I really have a fear of success, after all? Had my professor been trying to tell me something? I began looking deeper at what I might be fearful about: Is it the fact that 90 percent of my students were going to be older than I am? Am I too young to teach? Am I too inexperienced, incompetent, or just plain inadequate? The question of race concerned me, as well. Quickly, I began to second-guess everything—specifically my T.A.G.S. (talents, abilities, gifts, and skills.) I nearly drove myself crazy with negative self-talk and the vision of me, a young black male, teaching older, white students in Minnesota! What had I been thinking? My insecurities grew into a list:

1. *What if my students know more about the subject than I do?*

2. *What if I really cannot break down and explain the theories and concepts in the class textbook?*

3. *What if I am not prepared?*

4. *What if I cannot answer the students' questions?*

5. *What if I am not as smart and talented as I think I am?*

6. *What if they disagree with my grading policy just as I did as a student?*

7. *What if my students respond badly to my teaching style?*

8. *What if I lose my thoughts right in the middle of a lecture?*

9. *What if I am boring?*

Since then, I have come to accept many things about myself—especially the importance of being truthful. I was afraid and my professor had been right. I was afraid of my own success because I also feared my ability to sustain success once it was achieved. Once I owned my doubts, insecurities and fears, however, I was able to move beyond them.

If you allow the fear of success to reign supreme in your life, you will never know what you can become in life. Knowing the greatness of your T.A.G.S. is one of the surest ways to boost your self-concept and give back to the universe. You can actually bless and contribute to your generation when you tap into your human resources and celebrate them. Renowned psychologist Abraham Maslow coined self-awareness as "self-actualization"—inborn drive to develop all one's talents and capabilities. It involves understanding psychologically and emotionally your potential, as well as accepting others as unique individuals.

I had been afraid to own all of my talents, gifts, abilities and skills because I wasn't certain I truly deserved what I had achieved. Only after genuinely accepting that my success was the result of hard work was I able to move forward. Many individuals like myself, who come from disadvantaged childhoods and then find themselves achieving their dreams, don't often enjoy what they have achieved. We don't fear failure, we fear success.

Honor all that you have accomplished! Celebrate the results of your efforts! Take the time it takes (which can be years) to examine with honesty what might be holding you back from achieving your dream profession, relationship, or life. Is it the fear of failure—or, possibly, the fear of your own success?

Jermaine M. Davis

SUCCESS STRATEGIES
OF SIMON SAYS

S imon says...read on!

The games we played as children taught us many simple, basic lessons on how to play with others, build relationships and navigate the rules of childhood. Not only did they teach us about life, but the games we played as children were part of our life—the fun part. "Hide-n-Go Seek," "Kick-the-Can," and "Red Rover," all bring back the positive feelings of carefree afternoons, silliness and joy.

Do you remember your favorite hiding spot? Do you recall getting hit in the head with a recently kicked tomato soup can? Can you picture yourself hanging on the arms of two neighborhood friends determined not to let you break through?

Your mind still holds those memories, snapshots of play. We all have them somewhere. It's one of the common threads of being a child—our shared game playing. We also share the "rules" of the games we played as children, some of which have become ingrained in our very being—hard to recognize, and even harder to let go! Unfortunately, these "rules" may not serve any of us well in our adult years. Are you ready to visit the core lessons of one of your favorite childhood games; or, are you waiting for Simon to say...read on!

Old Rule: Catch people screwing up and throw them out of the game. No matter how hard you work, there will always be people who criticize you. By making you feel badly, they will somehow feel better. After a while, the weight of their negativity starts impacting your attitudes and energy. Most people thrive on positive—not negative, reinforcement. Are you caught up in "pleasing" Simon (i.e. not screwing up) so you can simply stay in the game?

New Rule: Catch people doing something well. Catching people doing something well should be a continuous process. You should not wait until the task is completed. Reward people along the way. You do not always get the right outcome on the first attempt.

Like teaching a toddler to walk, we are delighted when they crawl, then progress to standing with our help. Soon they stand on their own, even managing a step or two before falling down—which still solicits applause. Wouldn't it be nice if we were all acknowledged along the way for our efforts? Punishment is not terribly motivating.

Think about the many "Simons" in your life: a boss, parent, religious leader, peer, etc. Some of these people believe the way to influence people is through fear and intimidation. In the short term this can be an effective approach. In the long term, it loses its appeal. The best way to motivate others is to empower them. Encourage them to take risks. Praise. Show your appreciation. Say "thank you." Reward people around you for doing something well.

Old Rule: One mistake and you are out of the game. In Simon Says you don't get any second chances. Make a mistake or think differently from Simon, and you are out! The likely winners of the childhood game are those most like Simon. Unfortunately, many people—including you—may choose to believe you have to do what Simon would do to keep your job, be promoted, or be liked and accepted. The message is clear: It's my way or the highway!

New Rule: Warriors take risks; worriers are risks! Are you a worrier? A worrier is not something many people aspire to become. Nonetheless, most of us worry about our kids, lack of time to do everything we need to do, other's opinions of us, the stock market, whether it's going to rain...even worrying about worrying too much! Do you?

When you are so worried about making a mistake, or trying to please the "Simons" in your life, you behave in ways that are counterproductive to your own values. You begin to play it safe, or worry about the consequences of a future event. Worrying is a by-product of fear. You can't control everything that happens in your life, only how you respond. To live with worry and fear robs you of your ability to live in the present.

Try to control those things you can control by becoming a warrior! Focus on what is happening at the moment. Be less concerned about what happened in the past (which you can't undo) or about future events (which you can't predict.) Realize making mistakes is essential to your future success. If you are too afraid to think outside the box, you may end up trapped in it!

Old Rule: Do as I say, not as I do. One technique "Simon" uses to get people out of the game is to say one thing and do something completely different. This causes a great deal of confusion and leaves people feeling bitter. Have you ever justified an inappropriate act or remark by saying to your children, "Do as I say, not as I do?" You tell them not to smoke, for example, as you light up. You let your guests drive home after drinking at your home, yet tell your children about the harmful consequences of drinking and driving. Imagine how different things become when our actions and our words are consistent. People—including co-workers, community members, friends and your children—will always remember what you do over what you say.

New Rule: Say what you mean, mean what you say, and don't say it mean. Consider the distinction between what you intend and how your intentions affect others. For example, someone steps on your foot and accidentally hurts you. Although he didn't intend to hurt you, your foot is still throbbing. Just because he apologized doesn't mean your foot doesn't hurt. You are in pain! Likewise, accept responsibility for your actions, regardless of your intent. Know that pain is pain, whether physical or emotional.

You can make people hurt in many ways.

Old Rule: Just because everyone is doing the same thing doesn't make it the right thing. In the game of Simon Says, the orders are given so quickly that participants have little time to react. When unsure of what to do, they look around to see what others are doing so they can then do the same thing, and not be "out." What if the people you choose to follow don't know more than you know? What if the person you are following is thinking, "I must be going in the right direction because so many people are following me?" It takes far less energy to go with the crowd than to think on your own.

New Rule: Respond, don't react. The difference between response and reaction is thought. Most human beings have said something reactively which they would not have said had they thought about it for a moment. When you don't think before you speak, the results can be devastating.

Slow down! Take the time to reflect and ponder. Give yourself room to respond appropriately—not quickly. Take a deep breath. Calm down and step away. Give yourself some distance—maybe a night to sleep on it, or a week to get back to someone.

Another strategy for avoiding reactionary responses is to remember the word "BAR." The letter "B" reminds you to breathe. Deep breathing will center you, and prevent a knee jerk reaction. The letter "A" asks you to acknowledge what the other person is saying. When people are afraid to make a mistake, you can create a sense of safety by acknowledging their perspective. Keep in mind that acknowledging someone else's perspective doesn't necessarily mean that you agree with her. Finally, the letter "R" reminds you to respond through thought, not a "gut" instinct which is void of filtering. However, too often in stressful situations we do the process in reverse; instead of responding we REACT! When this occurs we say or do things we may later regret. Secondly, instead of acknowledging we ATTACK! We get defensive and go on the offensive resulting in the breakdown of communication. And finally, after we attack, we are so out of breath...we must BREATHE! This process can be the difference between enhancing your relationship through understanding and tearing apart your relationship through offensive behavior. Decisions based on a thinking response will almost always be better.

Simon Says is a simple game with simple lessons. Learning how to replace old rules with new rules will enhance the quality of your life—from your relationships, to sense of purpose—and everything in between. Play just to play. Laugh just to laugh. Simon says... have fun and never take the game of life too seriously!

Dr. Maura Cullen

SUCCESS...WHAT'S THAT?

*"...remember the Dick-and-Jane books and the first
word you learned—the biggest word of all—LOOK."*

- Robert Fulghum

Our son Ryan is two years old and is constantly pointing to different objects with an expression filled with excitement and curiosity. In a loud voice he'll ask, "What's that?" The answer we give is important because we know this is how he's learning about the world around him. As he gets older, it's a question we hope he'll never stop asking, because through that question he'll discover, learn, grow, and be successful. Our wish for our son—and anyone reading these words—is to never stop asking questions which allow you to discover, learn, and grow. Have you ever wondered about success? More specifically, have you ever wondered how to get it?

*"If a man does not keep pace with his companions, perhaps it
is because he hears a different drummer. Let him step to the
music which he hears, however measured or far away."*
- Henry David Thoreau

Be Yourself. Walter Payton was my favorite football player when I was growing up. I used to watch highlights of his games and then go to the practice field and pretend to be him. I wore his number on my uniform and wrapped tape around my cleats the way he did. One day at practice my coach blew the whistle and called me to the sideline. He told me to stop trying to run the ball like Walter Payton. "The only way to be successful in this game and in life," he said, "is to develop your own style and maximize your strengths. Trying to be someone else not only hurts you, but the entire team." I followed this advice in high school and found success—on and off the playing field.

In her book, *Reflections on the Art of Living: A Joseph Campbell Companion,* Diane Osbon uses the story of Sir Galahad to emphasize the importance of following our own paths. "The knights agree to go off on a quest... Each knight enters the forest at a mysterious point and follows his own intuition... When any knight sees the trail of another, thinks he's getting there, and starts to follow the other's track, he goes astray entirely."

In order to be successful, the knights would trust their own instincts and be true to themselves. Renowned psychiatrist Viktor Frankl, who spent years in Nazi concentration camps, said, "...everything can be taken from us but one thing: the last of human freedoms—to choose one's attitude in any given set of circumstances—to choose one's own way."

"For there is nothing either good or bad, but thinking makes it so." - William Shakespeare

Be Positive. Everything we do in our lives we do twice: first in our minds, and then in our actions. Our attitudes are incredibly powerful because they influence our choices and decisions. People often say to me, "I know how important it is to have a positive attitude, but how can I stay positive in the face of life's challenges?" There are five things we can do every day to maintain a positive attitude.

Surrounding ourselves with positive people is the first step in maintaining a positive attitude. Next to our faith and values, the company we keep is a powerful influence. Unfortunately, we're not always in complete control of our environments; and we can't control when those around us are being negative. No matter what's going on, we need to make a conscious effort, in our minds, to step away from negative people. This doesn't mean we stop listening to the people around us rather let their negative words affect us less.

Imagine how freeing it would be if a positive attitude were

like a giant oak tree, its roots deeply grounded and centered and its branches flexible enough to let others' negativity pass through. Don Miguel Ruiz touches on this possibility in his book, *The Four Agreements;* "Nothing others do is because of you. What others say and do is a projection of their own reality, their own dream. When you are immune to the opinions and actions of others, you won't be the victim of needless suffering."

When people are being negative, it's not about us; it's about them. Great leaders maintain their positive attitudes not only by surrounding themselves with positive people, but by not taking things personally when others are negative. That's the second step in maintaining a positive attitude. For instance, Dr. King had a vision for the planet; a place where people would not be "judged by the color of their skin, but by the content of their character." Despite knowing others didn't share this same hope, he believed in his vision. Likewise, Nelson Mandela refused to allow other's opinions dictate his beliefs, choices and actions. He led the fight against apartheid while serving a twenty-seven year prison sentence.

Surrounding ourselves with inspiring words, images, and music is the third way to maintain a positive attitude. When I ask my audiences, "How many of you have a dream vacation you'd like to go on?" All of the hands in the audience go up. I then ask, "How many of you have a picture or poster of that dream vacation hanging in your home or office?" Less than ten percent of the hands stay up as the rest go down.

The folks with their hands still up are much more likely to go on their dream vacations. What you focus on in your life is what you attract. For example, if I walked into your home, apartment, or office, would I see pictures of your goals and dreams? Have you considered creating a collage or montage of pictures as reminders of what you're focused on achieving? There are many successful people who have applied this particular visual strategy. Oprah Winfrey faced many challenges while growing up in an abusive household. To overcome these obstacles she surrounded herself with inspiring books that took her to wonderful places in her mind. Jim Carrey worked as a janitor while living in a car with his family, before he found success. Late one night in a coffee shop he drew a picture of an imaginary paycheck. On the check he wrote, "Pay to the order of Jim Carrey—ten million dollars." He kept it in his pocket and looked at it three or four times a day. Less than five years later, he was offered ten million dollars for a starring role in *The Mask 2,* the sequel to his popular film *The Mask.*

To summarize, surrounding ourselves with positive people and things, and trying to be a plus in the face of negativity are three ways to maintain a more positive attitude. Being more aware on a daily basis of how we're sitting, standing, walking and using our facial expressions is the fourth.

For instance, we've come to know our bodies often reflect our emotions, but can't it also be true that what we do with our bodies contributes to our emotions? Studies have shown our facial expressions have a direct influence on how we feel. Carol Tavris states, "When people are told to smile and look pleased or happy, their positive feelings increase; when they are told to look angry, displeased, or disgusted, positive feelings decrease." How we express ourselves physically plays a huge role in how we feel. As you continue reading this essay, be conscious of your body.

The fifth step for maintaining a positive attitude: finding humor in life's challenging moments. What have been the more challenging moments in your life—an unexpected traffic jam, delayed flight, temper tantrum from your child at a restaurant, or perhaps a surprise quiz in English class? These circumstances can cause a whole range of emotions from anger and sadness to complete frustration. But we have the power to choose how we respond to the situations and events in our lives.

I remember waiting for a flight from Boston to Chicago delayed three times due to weather. After I'd waited for four hours in the terminal, the flight was finally canceled. Many of the passengers were angry. As frustrated travelers stormed around the terminal, I looked at the passenger next to me and we both started to laugh. The weather and the decision to cancel the flight were out of our hands. The only thing we could control was our response. By finding humor in the moment we maintained our positive attitudes while others chose to be negative. We may not always be in control of our circumstances, but we are always in control of our reactions.

"'What's the world's greatest lie?' the boy asked, completely surprised. 'It's this: that at a certain point in our lives, we lose control of what's happening to us, and our lives become controlled by fate. That's the world's greatest lie.'" - Paulo Coelho, The Alchemist

Be Committed. To be successful in life, being ourselves and being positive are not always enough. We have to be clear on what we want and be committed to taking actions towards our goals, otherwise our wants and desires are just wishful thinking. Fast Company, a popular magazine among business leaders, did a survey to determine the most important qualities successful leaders possess. The most common response was the ability to take action and commit to a goal, idea, or project. Create a vision for your life that answers the questions: Where do I want to go? Who do I want to be? What am I passionate about?

During my junior year of college, I was offered an opportunity to go into a lucrative business venture. It was a big risk requiring me to drop out of school, give up my involvements and move back home, leaving my friends and social life behind. I never stopped to think about whether this was the right path for me or if I was passionate about the idea. I took the risk.

Two months later, the business venture folded. I had left school, was out of a job and started to doubt myself. I was scared about what I should do next. It was my dad who helped me break through this challenging time. He told me, "Life will continue to bring you challenges, and when you overcome one there will always be another. The key is to be clear on what you want and where you want to go. Be committed, learn from your mistakes, and face any obstacle with courage."

During the weeks following that conversation I spent a lot of time thinking about where I wanted to go, and created a plan for getting my life back on track. I went back to school, increased my course load to graduate on time, reconnected with my friends, and started a business. You can achieve your goals too by asking your-self the same questions found in this six-step formula for success!

Six-Step Formula for Success:

1. What goals do you want to achieve?

2. How can you make each of your goals recognizable so you'll know when they've been achieved?

3. What resources or skills do you currently possess that will help you reach your goals?

4. What mini-goals do you need to get started?

5. By what date do you want to accomplish each of the above mini-goals?

6. By what date do you want to achieve each of your major goals?

To be successful we have to be clear on where we want to go and what we want to achieve. We need to be so committed we never settle for mediocrity. It's not just about the goal, but who we become as we strive to achieve it.

"Do one thing every day that scares you." - *Eleanor Roosevelt*

Be Curious. The last recommended way to achieve success is to be curious. Several years ago, I took a trip to Alaska with some friends. I went because it was a once in a lifetime opportunity. We visited Mount McKinley, also known as Denali "The Great One." At 20,320 feet, Denali is the tallest mountain in North America and is regarded as one of the largest single mountains in the world. It is about four times as high as the Grand Canyon is deep and is about as tall as five Golden Gate bridges strung end to end. In its presence I was reminded of how big the world is and how much more there is to see and do.

As I looked at the "Great One" I realized being successful is not an object or a thing; rather, success is about creating moments, and those moments come from being curious. Someone once said, "Life is not measured by the number of breaths we take, but by the number of moments that take our breath away." These moments are different for everyone. It could be a trip to Alaska with friends, swimming with dolphins, watching a sunset, or experiencing the birth of your child...the list goes on and on.

As you discover, learn and grow, keep asking yourself the big questions—the ones with big answers! Begin with the biggest question of all, "What's that?" then follow the four steps outlined above: Be yourself. Be positive. Be committed. Be curious.

Ed Gerety

WOMEN: IT'S TIME TO CELEBRATE!

"If success is not on your own terms, if it looks good to the world but does not feel good in your heart, it is not success at all."

- Anna Quindlen

It's time to celebrate. Mine may be a quiet voice, but I believe it is time to celebrate what women bring to our society.

Too often, we measure the worth and accomplishments of individuals by yardsticks which are easily quantifiable: How much money they earned, the positions they held in business, the level of positions to which they were elected, the net worth of their companies, the size of their office or home. In this set of measurements, corporate moguls are more valuable than teachers, surgeons are more valuable than homemakers, and astronauts are more valuable than Boy Scout pack leaders. These measures almost automatically devalue the work and role of women.

Yes! It's time to celebrate! It is time to celebrate women who touch and enrich the lives of others; to celebrate women who have visions of improving our society and take action to make their visions reality; to celebrate women who rise above physical, financial and emotional adversity to build happy lives for themselves and their children; to celebrate women who through their voluntary service to their churches and civic organizations make our communities safer, more literate and more joyful. These are the women who should be both celebrated and memorialized.

What women do you celebrate? Are you proud of your accomplishments and priorities? Do you acknowledge the successful women in your life and seek ways to build up young women? There can never be enough gratitude shared among women for our many strengths and contributions to society. It's time to celebrate!

As one of the few female college presidents in the country, I am blessed to interact with women making remarkable contributions to the world. Let me mention a few women who deserve recognition for what they have done as individuals—and the many other women they represent. Go ahead, talk about them, too!

An English major at the University of Delaware, Carrieri Russo is the co-founder of Success Won't Wait, a non-profit group that collects books and distributes them to schools, libraries, community gathering spots and U.S. soldiers serving in Iraq. She was recognized as one of five national winners of the Jefferson Awards, the Jacqueline Kennedy Onassis Award for Outstanding Public Service Benefiting Local Communities.

One of the world's foremost ornithologists, Roxie Laybourne, spent most of her career at the Smithsonian Institution in Washington, D.C. She solved mysteries from murders to plane crashes using feathers as her clues. She saved the whooping crane by inventing an instrument which allows scientists to identify the gender of cranes. Laybourne was a consultant for the FBI, Pratt and Whitney, General Electric and the Federal Aviation Administration until her death in 2003 at age 92.

A kindergarten teacher at Broad Acres Elementary School in Silver Spring, Maryland, Kimberly Oliver was named the 2006 National Teacher of the Year. "There's a quality that can't be measured in this profession—one that makes it the art form that it really is," said her boss, Montgomery County schools chief Jerry D. Weast. "And Kim has that quality—of doing the right thing at the right time in the right way, of making every child feel special. And she does it all without lowering expectations."

While a student at Central Michigan University, Ashley

Radawski attended a session of LeaderShape, a program designed to encourage leading with integrity. She created a vision to expand international assistance to people in need. She focused on those in Vietnam who are still being affected by the war. She also wanted to educate her peers on the current issues which are affecting millions. Ashley has created a group on campus, and is planning a service outreach trip to Vietnam in future summers. They are well on their way to funding this initiative. Because of Ashley's efforts, 10 Central Michigan University students will travel to Vietnam to do community service and present a donation to aid in the cleanup of land mines.

A Junior League member from Macon, Georgia, Carmen Herndon has made several trips to New Orleans to help rebuild homes damaged by Hurricane Katrina. Her dedication encouraged other members of the Junior League of Macon to join her. She plans to return because the work is not finished.

Throughout her career as an attorney, judge, and human rights activist, Sharin Ebadi has been a passionate advocate for justice, women and children's rights, and peace. That she does all of this in Iran, where she receives death threats and is constantly watched by the government, makes her work, courage, and dedication, that much more remarkable. Ebadi won the Nobel Peace Prize in 2004 for her work.

As the first person in her family to attend college, Teresa Nichols struggled as a first-generation student and had to work multiple jobs. She not only became the first person in her family to graduate from college, she studied abroad, was a campus leader, and graduated in four years. After graduation, she took time from a successful career to work with students who were at risk because of their socio-economic situations.

I bring these women forward as women we should celebrate! I cannot tell you the stories of all remarkable women, but I can tell you about a few who represent the whole. All of these women have led remarkable lives and each is a woman of achievement representing great diversity. They represent a range of family incomes; they studied or are studying fields from biology to law, and their birth dates span over 75 years. You have to search beneath the surface to find their common traits.

What do these women have in common?

"...it has always proved that the grandeur of a nation was shown by the respect paid to women." - *Clara Barton, 1902*

Characteristics of Successful Women:

- Full participation in life

- An understanding that their education made them women of privilege with a responsibility to society

- Experience in working in groups and teams

- A commitment to serving others

- The self-confidence to try things that had not been done and the willingness to work hard to make things happen

What can we learn from these women? What lessons do they teach us? Each defines success by their own terms—not through someone else. They care about others and act on that concern. Their actions enrich our communities. I invite women everywhere to take the time to celebrate the work and success of other women—career women, community volunteers, stay-at-home moms, activists, church leaders, and entrepreneurs.

Women born since the end of World War II have been faced with opportunities, options and challenges that earlier generations never experienced. They have also faced a changing set of societal values that slide every few years. The baby boom generation has lived through the Super Mom Syndrome (you can be a perfect spouse, career woman and mother all at the same time), the Glass Ceiling (you can move up the career ladder but the top rung is not accessible to you), the Mommy Track (you are moved off the fast track if you choose to have children), the Martha Stewart Phenomenon (you should be able to create a world class garden, whip up creative handiwork from scraps around the house, cook gourmet meals and run a publishing empire while looking unhurried), and the Lawrence Sommers Theory (you are just not as capable as men in math and science).

What's next? My observations suggest we may be heading back to Super Mom, again. Only this time with a new twist...

It's time to celebrate! It's time to own our individuality and the many diverse contributions which make women successful. If we truly embrace the notion of communities with women who serve as corporate CEO's and chauffeurs for their children, ministers and marines, deans and pack leaders, elementary teachers and engineers, secretaries and sociologists, fire fighters and factory workers, pilots and *Pilates* instructors—then we must accept and celebrate their differences, and their definitions of success.

Dr. Maureen A. Hartford

Thinking Differently

ABUNDANCE THINKING

Nothing is ever what it seems and everything that glitters isn't necessarily authentic gold or diamonds. As human beings we are socialized into believing certain things, only to discover a completely different reality.

Take the "class clown" from your elementary school days, for example, who turns out to be a brilliant comedian; or the classmate from high school voted "less likely" to succeed who ends up becoming a millionaire. Think about the next door neighbor who wants you to believe her marriage is picture perfect, yet you hear the fighting and screaming night after night; or the friend who constantly makes jokes about her parenting skills when you know his child is in trouble.

Reality versus perception—which is real? More importantly, which do you want to be real? When you continually put images or wear masks for others to see, consider who is really being fooled. Allowing your colleagues, neighbors, classmates, and friends, to love you for your strengths and weaknesses is a powerful human condition. When you reveal that which is real, you open the door for genuine responses, care and compassion.

We all have struggles, and bad things happen to good people. This is life. Some people seem better equipped to handle their realities, while others continue to disguise or hide their problems, struggles and challenges hoping if they don't acknowledge them (or pass them off as something else) they simply don't exist. Denial is an individual's attempt to escape reality. What you resist only persists!

However, when you desire truth, and want to accept your reality, you can move on and do it what it takes to fix what's broken in your world—either way life goes on. Why not eliminate the chaos interfering with your success? A commitment to self-improvement will move you forward. There is much to gain by taking inventory of your life—the good and bad, the happy and sad, the hope and the despair. It's time to make a decision; to either think with abundance, or to fall back on the more self-absorbed and unproductive mind-set of scarcity.

Abundant people (who might have plenty of reasons to be unhappy) live with abundance thinking. This is the process of accurately seeing your place in the world as one of purpose and meaning. Although by other's standards, you are "justified" in being miserable, angry and depressed, thinking from the perspective of abundance forces you to direct your life and control that which you can control. You choose to proceed with hope, not hopelessness.

With abundance thinking you give of your time and talents, and in return you receive happiness, satisfaction and a sense of self-worth. You approach the challenges in your life as part of a Divine Plan and know there are always those who have considerably less than you. Even in despair, you look for ways to reach out to others who need your support and compassion. Your world isn't about blame, self-pity, denial and defeat. You live in a real world where people do suffer, yet survive.

Scarcity thinking people share many of the unfortunate realities of abundant thinking people, yet have chosen to think differently about their world. They refrain from enjoying the joy, seeking fellowship, and accepting the meaning that is their life. Instead, they focus on the unproductive question: Why me? They operate using scarcity thinking, or a mind-set based upon limited resources and "not enough to go around" thinking. Caught up in their own issues, struggles and challenges, they are unable to look at a bigger picture calling them to step back and focus on the lightness within their darkness.

From which mind-set do you operate—from which reality?

Try out a few abundance thinking behaviors, and see if you begin to notice all that you have, instead of all that is missing in your life!

1. Consider that there is enough pie for everyone to have dessert.

2. Realize that the Creator has freely given T.A.G.S. (talents, abilities, gifts, and skills) to each person on planet Earth.

3. Embrace, respect, and welcome those who develop their T.A.G.S. and show those who can't find their T.A.G.S. how to see them.

4. Stay on track by supporting a friend in need who is going through a tough time.

5. Give away possessions to people who need them more than you do (Clean out your closets every six months.)

6. Thank those who have been around during your dark days, and those who have supported your efforts.

7. Make a list of your blessings every day.

8. Bring meals to your neighbors when they least expect it.

9. Never doubt words of encouragement and praise are always appreciated.

Nothing is ever what it seems. As human beings we are socialized into believing one thing, only to discover a completely different reality. When you consciously try to think with abundance, your perceptions and your realities become the same. What you put out there for others to see, is your true self—whether in pain, celebration, defeat or confusion. Choose abundant thinking—choose happiness!

Jermaine M. Davis

BE REAL

Ever have those days? Or those people in your life? You know the ones: They challenge your abilities, question who you thought you were, and force you to examine your motives. Although "those people" may cause turmoil, disappointment and insecurity in your life, they often make you stronger as a result.

Early in my career, I had an experience with a difficult co-worker. He was undermining my efforts, speaking negatively about me with co-workers, misrepresenting my work, and took every opportunity to publicly disagree with my opinion. Despite being upbeat and enthusiastic in the pursuit of my success, this individual was definitely bringing me down. He was clearly out to get me. Others noticed his behavior, as well.

One morning, I came into my office to find a card on my desk from a sympathetic co-worker and friend. The card simply read: "Be real." I remember reading the card and wondering why my friend had chosen those particular words. Why not go with sentiments like, "Hang in there!" or "Take the high road?" I kept asking myself, "Why did I have to 'be real' when I wasn't wrong?"

Eventually, I figured out the answer. The key to working with my sabotaging colleague was to focus less on him, and more on me! Not in a selfish way, rather by focusing on the true me, I would achieve my goals regardless of his behavior. By asking myself questions like, "How can I use my skills to meet this challenge?" rather than getting worked up over the conflict, I would be practicing helpful communication skills, admitting my apprehensions and dedicating myself to my future success.   Eleanor Roosevelt once said, "People can't make you feel inferior without your consent." Once I realized I was giving away my power, I was able to more truthful and real about my fears—I was becoming more of an authentic person.

To be true, you must be the person you know you are—despite what others may say or do. What does this mean? You must possess clarity of self and raw honesty about your values, passions and purpose in life. This clarity gives you the freedom to live without being bothered by others' negative intentions. In short, the note on my desk was a challenge to stay on my own course, hold on to my beliefs, and not let one individual tell me who I am. Only I can do that.

The challenge of figuring out what it means to be real with ourselves and others remains. It is a different challenge for each of us and a lifelong process of discovering who you are and what matters most in your life.

Dr. Lori Hart Ebert

BE THE CABOOSE

Undeniably, the engine is the sexiest car on the train. It gets the best paint job, it is the car people don't get to ride in, and it is the part that makes the train run. Whether or not this engine is fed by coal, gas or electricity, it is what collectors covet the most, and when a train goes racing by, it is the engine that catches your eye.

My favorite car, however, isn't the engine. It's the caboose. Without it, the rest of the train can come off the track—even the engine. It is a strong and focused workhorse. It doesn't need to be in front. The caboose makes sure the rest of the cars make it safely to their destination. The caboose is also special for it carries presidents and movie stars who stand on its back end. From this desirable position, they waive, give speeches and chug down the tracks able to see where they have been.

Think about where you work, or an organization you belong to, or your community. What part of the train are you? How do you see your contribution?

I work in higher education where the academic mission is the engine. Anyone who works at a college or university is defined by that particular mission. It is what defines us, like a custom paint job. The students are the cars—hopefully, headed somewhere and with purpose.

What part of the train am I? That's right...the caboose! Specifically, the "non-academic" part of the train called "student affairs." I know I'm not the engine and that's okay with me. When I look down the track, I see a desired destination ahead—sometimes before the conductor sees it. I see potential train wrecks (often before they happen), along with crashes and "stuff" falling on the tracks.

I may chug along without a lot of fanfare or pomp and circumstance, but I know that I am valued. I know everyone plays a role in the train getting from one place to another. Without the caboose, a train wouldn't be a train. The caboose would be missed.

Are you the best you can be at what you do? Are you showing off your pride by doing great work, or do you whine at your lack of recognition? Self-esteem is at the heart of the beholder. You will make a greater contribution to your work, organization, and family, for instance, when you feel your contribution is great. Go ahead, be the best caboose ever!

Laura De Veau

BORING PEOPLE

"Boredom is not a state of mind.
Boredom is the state of not using your mind."
- Nancy Hunter Denney

How many times have you heard someone complain about being bored? How many times has a friend mentioned she has nothing to do? Worse yet, how does it feel after seeing (and paying for) what you thought was a great movie preceded by a wonderful meal, to have your date comment on the way home, "I'm bored."

Despite the fact you'd probably welcome ten minutes in your day to simply "be bored," if you had ten extra minutes, wouldn't you choose something more exciting than boredom? Wouldn't you call someone, visit a friend, say a prayer, read your favorite magazine, or play a quick game of cards? You'd find a way to use your precious ten minutes, wouldn't you?

With all there is to do in this world, I don't understand how people with so much potential can be bored. This is why I've come to the conclusion: People who are bored are most likely boring people! It's not that there isn't anything to do it's that you can't think of anything to do. Your energy is being spent blaming the external source(s) of your discontent, as opposed to focusing on what attitude shift, or energy expenditure is needed to bring you more personal satisfaction.

Sure, there are times when we all get bored. For example, you choose the wrong movie, find yourself standing in a grocery line too long, or stay on hold with your phone company listening to the number of minutes that will pass before your call can be answered. These are excusable because they are understandable, and the way you are spending your time has been taken out of your control (for the most part). You were anticipating a reasonable time frame, and got something much different. You weren't prepared to fill this gap with more constructive behavior than waiting.

So, when you can control your time; do things to lift your spirits, bring happiness to others or challenge your intellect. Do things which improve your skills, add to your knowledge of the world, and make you a more interesting person. Decide to visit an interesting place, research your options, and make the arrangements to go, but not with a boring friend! There are so many wonderful things to do in this world, interesting places to visit, and fascinating people to meet—if only you had the time.

You can find fascination in your immediate surroundings, as well. If you find yourself getting discouraged by the expense of foreign travel, or the president wasn't able to clear his schedule for you today, find fun at home. Look through your high school year book, offer to baby-sit your neighbor's kids, or write a letter to yourself (date it ten years from now.) Go see a movie with subtitles, become a volunteer in a local literacy agency, invite someone who would least expect it over for coffee, rearrange your furniture, put your pictures in an album, arrange your CDs in alphabetical order, or take a walk.

When contemplating boredom, your only choice is to ask; am I boring? If the answer is yes, or you want a higher level of self-esteem than accepting boring as a personality characteristic, you must act! Go do something—anything, but don't stay in one place announcing your lack of curiosity, questioning, intrigue, aptitude and potential. Don't look to your teacher, professor, friends, or parents to make your life exciting. That's your job! Do you really want to be known as *boring?*

Judson Laipply

DO IT WITH "CLASS"

Class is respect for others. It's a deep and genuine respect for every human being, regardless of status.

Class does not require money, status, success, or ancestry. The wealthy aristocrat may not even know the meaning of the word, yet the poorest man in town may radiate class in everything he does.

Class is having manners. It is always saying "thank you" and "please." It is complimenting people for any and every task that is done well.

Class is treating others as you want them to treat you.

Class is never making excuses for one's own shortcomings, rather using one's failures to learn important life lessons, and bounce back from mistakes.

Class is never bragging or boasting about one's own accomplishments, and never tearing down or diminishing the achievements of another person.

Class is self-respect.

Class is how you see yourself in comparison to the world.

If you have class, you don't have to tell anyone. They already know.

Rick Barnes

FIRST THINGS FIRST

It was a big night a few years ago—our first father-daughter dance, sponsored by my daughter Bethany's high school. Dressed to kill (more her than me,) we went to dinner at a hotel before the dance. We drove my car downtown and pulled up to the hotel front door. The young doormen seemed to trip over themselves to greet us! But I'm sure neither my car or I were the main attraction.

They gave me a valet parking ticket and ushered us into the hotel. We had a great evening—a father and a daughter together—enjoying the meal and each other.

As dinner ended, it was time to leave the hotel for the big dance. We got our coats and went through the lobby to the front door. As I reached for the valet ticket, the doorman smiled and pointed; he already had my car there, at the curb! They tripped over each other again opening the door for Bethany, while I took some cash from my wallet to reward them for the great service.

As I handed him the tip, the valet attendant hesitated. He looked to the doorman for some direction. Apparently, the car had never been moved the car from where I left it because the valet didn't know how to drive a stick-shift! Some great service.

"If you're going to do a job, you'd better learn the basics—first things first!" I offered. Then, I left my daughter at the curb for a few minutes while I gave the valet for a brief driving lesson around the parking lot!

Dr. Dennis Black

GET IT RIGHT
THE FIRST TIME

The day after college graduation, my dad laughed as he cut up my gas credit card. This was the only credit card I had in college. My dad knew what he was doing. He was saying: "You are on your own—starting now! Go make some money and start paying for your own basic needs!" Message received.

Where do you get money when you suddenly find yourself on your own? Apparently, you need to earn it. Of course, I always knew this day would come, but I didn't think it meant that I actually needed to get a job! Where do you begin? Where is the road map to your future?

I truly believe that if you know what you want to do, someone will hire you to do it. Not only do you begin by articulating what type of position you seek, but your resume must also clearly express this goal. Your wardrobe also needs to emphasize your intent while keeping in line with realistic expectations.

If your only criteria for a job after college is to make up for the loss of your credit card, any job will do. That is, any job you can and will do. You can and should want to do better. Be intentional about your first job whether it is technically "professional" or not. Needing an income or having the luxury of finding the "perfect fit" the first time out, isn't the point. Seek a source of income fitting your desired career path, or one that can be a stepping stone to help you develop specific skills you will need later on.

I believe your first job after college has the potential to influence and even dictate your second, third and fourth jobs. So, how do you get it right the first time?

1. Start by identifying your aptitudes and interests; they are good indicators of your likely career path.

2. Work hard at everything you do. Demonstrate that you are reliable, capable and willing to take on new responsibility.

3. Be persistent in going after what you want. If one approach (like simply sending in your resume) doesn't work, find someone who has an inside contact. Use it!

4. Interview people currently holding a position you desire—what experience, credentials, or strategies did they employ? How did they get hired?

5. Continue to seek the right first job, while you earn money to pay the bills.

Dr. Lori Hart Ebert

I SHOULD

*"Those who have one foot in the canoe and
one foot on the shore are going to fall into the river."*

- Tuscarora Tribal Proverb

On a recent New Year's Eve, I made yet another resolution. I would delete the following from my vocabulary:

- "should"
- "but..."
- "I'll try"
- "if only..."
- and "I wish..."

As many resolutions go, a few months later, a few "shoulds" were being spoken, and "if only" was becoming a close friend.

In May, I was saved! A young woman crossed my path and reminded me to focus on what I wanted, and to be deliberate—not just wishful—about how I was going to achieve my goal. I was inspired! She spoke of her plan of moving from "I should" to "I might" to "I will." Intriguing.

Never being able to leave good enough alone, I expanded upon this type of "progression thinking" and ended up with a process to revive your plans, hopes and dreams that are filed under "S" for

Someday. Do you need to start working on your resolutions—again? Here's how it works...

"Do or do not, there is no try." - *Yoda, Jedi Master*

"I should!"

When you are in the "I should" mode, it is usually because you feel a sense of obligation or have made a promise to yourself, another person or group. You may be at this stage because you know the right course of action, and have yet to act. You want to be fulfilled, which is not compelling enough to cause you to make a move.

"I might!"

At the "I might" stage, you can picture the possibilities a little more clearly and see the probable positive results. You may express your "mights" out loud. This begins to make your thoughts real. In spite of verbalizing these ideas, you can be vulnerable here—you may doubt yourself and others may question your ability to accomplish what you are suggesting. Using "might" leaves your options too exposed, revealing a low level of commitment. It's easy to stay here because you are still thinking and hoping. Hope is good—it's not a plan!

"I can!"

When you say "I can!" to yourself and others, you are empowered to apply your skills and talents to a measurable course of action. You know how to access and use resources, people, money, time, materials and knowledge. You have increased your confidence level and are ready, willing and able to do what needs to be done.

"I will!"

You will because you must! There is an increased sense of urgency now and you have a plan with a timeline. Based on what you know you can do—or, can find out how to do—you put the stake in the ground and vow to take action.

"I am!"

"I am" is the here and now. You recognize that you are doing what you said you would. The joy of action replaces the fear of failure. When I was five years old, my Dad taught me to ride a bike on my school playground and I distinctly remember the feeling of incredible freedom once he let go. I got my balance and suddenly realized I was actually winding my way around the basketball hoops and jungle gyms, never again to use training wheels. I remember yelling out "I'm doing it, I'm doing it!" That sense of arrival, independence and relief still hits me when I recognize I am actually doing what I have set out to do.

"I did!"

"I did" evolves from "I am." Your accomplishments deserve celebration! So, when you find yourself saying, "I really should..." remember the power and pride that comes from being at "I did."

You are not done yet—now you can help others get past their "shoulds" and move to their own "dids." Sharing your success with others, as with all good deeds, comes back to you one-hundred fold.

Kristin Skarie

THE ROAD

*"One day while far away from home and on the road again,
I looked down and realized the pavement I was driving on was
literally connected to my driveway. It was just a matter of time and
distance. I never felt as homesick or as far away from home again."*

It has been my privilege to travel to every state in the United States of American and to many Provinces of Canada to speak on topics ranging from leadership, values, ethics, character driven decision making and conflict resolution, customer service, diversity, spirituality, and grieving. I have maintained relationships with my clients, become good friends with several of them, and in fact, as an Intercollegiate Chaplain, have married some of them to their significant others, baptized their children, and sadly, have even buried two of them long before they should have left our planet. As I write this I remember the memorial services at The University of Southern Mississippi for Dr. Tom Shoemaker, and the service at The University of Redlands in California for Neal Pahia. The Gospel Choir at Southern Miss sang Dr. Tom to Heaven while the Hawaiian students at Redlands sang and did the hula to take Neal's Spirit Home.

Being asked to speak; that is, to share knowledge, inspire, comfort the afflicted, and afflict the comfortable, is a great honor and a tremendous responsibility. I did not always know this. You see, there are different stages of being on the road, and with each stage comes a mind set and a new body of knowledge to be learned. This insight can best be learned experientially; but nonetheless, there is benefit in reading about it and conceptually understanding the road and its many lessons that will help you decide:

1. Should I go on the road and speak? And if the answer is Yes,

2. How do I do this with integrity, sanity, and keep my personal and family life intact?

Ah...the second part is the hard part. Many of the wonderful speakers I know who started out on the road as a pair—with a lover, partner, husband, or wife—are now one. That is; divorced, single again, and/or looking. I am still married to Donna Keim for 26 years and running, but the reality is that my vocation has in many ways made her a single parent responsible for her share, and many times mine, of the child raising responsibilities.

So we begin our time together with The Stages of Being on the Road—I do not presume to know all the stages, but I do know the ones that have shown themselves to me during my visits to 50 states, several Provinces, and my two and a half million miles on Delta Air Lines.

The Stages of Being on the Road:

Stage 1: "On the Road." The excitement of planning the first trip; the amazement that someone really wants you to speak and will pay you to do it! Statements such as, "I cannot believe how lucky I am. I have this amazing opportunity. Wow. They are paying me to talk. I'm only working an hour and a half a day. Is this legal? I am the luckiest person in the world." New sights, sound, places, restaurants, and people. This is the 'enthrallment' stage of public speaking and traveling. You are quite literally 'enchanted' by the road. And...the road knows this, for the road is a living thing with great insight if not a devious character.

Stage 2: "Road Warrior." You are now getting good at getting on the road and living there. "I've got this wired," you think. You know the short cuts. You know the rights roads and the best hotels. Packing is a breeze. You have learned to fold and roll your clothes to avoid wrinkles. You also begin to amass enough miles to upgrade to first class on the airplanes. Yeah baby! Bring it on. At this point you may even be flying all night to get to a lecture and give yourself 6 additional hours at home. You know now not to watch the in-flight movie early in the month and the check in folks at the airport and hotels know you by name. This is the honeymoon phase, enjoy it. It does not last forever.

Stage 3: "Road Kill." "What in the hell was I thinking?" "Do they ever change the movie on the planes or in the hotels?" "I am exhausted and I can't believe I scheduled myself like this." You begin to notice that everyone at home has gone on with their lives and there is not a celebration at the airport each time you get home. You still expect everyone to stop whatever they are doing at home and join in your joy at being home, but you notice that people have adjusted to the "Road Warrior" living amongst the mortals and simply function with, or sadly, without you. You begin to think about not getting on the plane or showing up. Many people give up here and I am willing to consider the possibility that these are the truly mentally healthy ones. Some of us go on.

Stage 4: "I am the Road, and the Road is Me." "You know that's interesting that you ask because I did consider getting a regular job again. I don't think I am cut out for normal work anymore. Three days in one place and I get antsy." You start to rise from the ashes like a Phoenix out of the road kill that was you and appreciate the benefits of traveling again, making a conscious decision to find beauty wherever you go and try to blend in at home and fit into their schedules. You accept the shuttle home instead of a ride and understand people have real things to do that do not necessarily center around you. Your life now includes the road, like it includes your lover, significant other, home, and children. It has become part of who you are; you may even send birthday cards now to flight attendants or the nice college student who waited on you in the restaurant in Mt. Vernon, Illinois.

Stage 5: "The Road is My Vocation." You finally understand that the road is truly where I am supposed to be and speaking is definitely what I am supposed to be doing. This is not my job; rather, it is my vocation. "I have seen the good I can do and now my work and my view of it is totally different." You have learned to be fully home when you are home and fully on the road when you are gone. You have also learned that a pizza eaten on the east coast at 11 p.m. is really eaten at 11 p.m. and you cannot count it as 8 p.m. because that is the time at home. You switch your watch to the new time on takeoff and experience a poetic vision of yourself as one called to travel, comfort and inform. Having survived Stage 3, you may even consider yourself what Father Nouwen called a "wounded healer."

You have learned the road's best kept and hardest to attain secret: BALANCE. It is all about balance. Life is about balance. Personal relationships are about balance; the balance of nature; the balance of a gymnast on the beam. You have learned to balance all the myriad important dimensions of your life, and somehow, it all makes sense, as if there was a plan, as if there was a director, offering you a path, a Tao, a road toward the amazing insight that we all have a gift, a place, and a purpose. You have received your initial degree from The University of the Road. The road looks back at you and beckons, "Just over this next hill. You should see what I can see. C'mon. Let's go."

It happened to me one day far away from my home in Oregon. Between stages and searching for the meaning and purpose of my travel, the road said to me, "Hey. Do you know that your driveway is connected to the road you are driving on right now?" I said, "What?" The road repeated, "The road you are on right now, the one your tires are rolling on, is directly connected to your driveway." I thought, "What an amazing insight." The road said, "Yeah, I know." And I never felt very far away from home again. "Thank you," I thought to the road. And the road said, "You're welcome. I thought you were ready to hear that."

Dr. Will Keim

MAKING YOUR REALITY

Don't you wish you could just "tune it all out" sometimes? Static kills. Sometimes we just need to take a break from the noise, to get back to the things that really matter to us. Are you stressed out? Join the club. We could all stand to relax—so why not make the choice to do that now?

Stress is all part of your environment. It is nothing more than perception. Stress is a ringing phone, a crashing computer, a dying car engine, a nagging parent, a prodding spouse, and a screaming child. Everything around us is a potential source of stress if we let it be so. But that's the key—"if we let it be so." Stress is a product of our surroundings, but once we feel that stress, we choose what to do with it! Following that logic, you can control your stress. You can choose not to feel it. Think your way to being calm.

Start seeing the world in terms of bigger of time. Think about hours, rather than minutes. Life looks a little more trivial in this light. The traffic jam that keeps you from getting home, the long line at the grocery store, the car double parked, or the delay of a flight might cause you stress. But when you think about their place in the bigger scheme of your week, month or lifetime, they're not as important! They become the small things again. Why let them control your emotions?

If you're not careful, stress will threaten your health. The more you stress about something, the more you'll suffer both the mental and physical effects of stress. But stress is in the eye of the beholder. Choose what "gets" to you. Whenever you can, laugh if off!

Find the humor in the situation. Switch your mind to a different station.

Or just take a break and tune out.

Judson Laipply

QUITTING TO WIN

By the third year of college I was a Jack-of-All-Trades. I was involved in about ten student organizations—an officer in half of them. In addition, I wrote a weekly column for the newspaper, trained for baseball, held a national position with a large organization, and worked about thirty hours a week.

Needless to say, I was overwhelmed. Letting go of things I enjoyed was hard, but necessary for my survival. I wanted more free time to enjoy my final year of college and I wanted to give one hundred percent. I also realized potential employers would not likely be impressed with the quantity of my activities, but rather with the willingness to devote my time and energy, along with the quality of my work.

Making these tough choices taught me an important lesson: Sometimes you have to quit to win. My senior year of college was great. I reduced my commitments, but the few organizations in which I was involved got a more committed leader. My weekly column was greatly improved, and I played the best baseball of my life! I was healthier, happier, and more well-rounded because I let go of the things that were bringing me down.

A few years later, in graduate school, I found myself in a familiar position. I had embarked on a speaking career. My goal was to speak frequently to a wide variety of audiences. Given my desire to act, I was also pursuing acting leads. Once again, I had spread myself too thin.

Emotionally torn between two wonderful opportunities, I knew a choice had to be made. The first was a speaking engagement in Washington, DC—which coincided with an audition in New York City! Instead of doing the right thing, I tried to do both.

I thought, "Don't burn any bridges!" And, off I went to New York City, despite leaving my heart in Washington, DC. Although I generated a few leads from my acting ability, I went to my agent and said, "I quit." What a moment of clarity!

I was now free to win. I was free to focus. I was free to get what I wanted. Temptation continued to pull me back to acting, pitting my ego against common sense. Having faith in my previous decision, I gracefully declined what appeared to be a wonderful acting job. Since then, I have had a rewarding speaking career.

Sometimes, even after deciding, you have to decide all over again.

Being a "Jack-of-All-Trades" and a master of none happens when you spread yourself too thin, ignore your true destiny and fail to focus on one goal at a time. Bottom line: Sometimes you have to quit in order to win!

Judson Laipply

Wisdom and Reflection

THE CALM BEFORE
THE BRAINSTORM

Nyelah is a successful executive in corporate America, where she has spent the last ten years in sales, marketing, and management. She doesn't feel fulfilled and has lost her desire to continue working in corporate America.

She pictures herself starting her own business and creating a powerful and well-respected company. The problem is that Nyelah doesn't know exactly what kind of business to pursue or how to narrow down her list of possibilities. She feels confused. Her mentor encourages her to brainstorm for three to five minute intervals on her entrepreneurial possibilities.

Nyelah finds a quiet place in her basement, grabs a legal pad and a green ballpoint pen (a fine-tipped one at that) and begins to think about her work experience, T.A.G.S. (talents, abilities, gifts and skills) and personal business interests. Each day she sets her stopwatch for three minutes and writes down the possible businesses she could start. She considers her T.A.G.S. and how they relate to her business interests.

Nyelah's brainstorming generates thirty-seven possible business ventures. From this list, she narrows her options and decides where to focus her energy. Nyelah makes a final decision after contemplating her personal values, T.A.G.S., business interests, and viable business opportunities.

What does Nyelah's story reveal about the practice of brainstorming and how it can help you achieve success?

Successful individuals know precisely what they want and can describe their goals in vivid and tangible detail. It doesn't matter what you want out of school, work or life, what matters is how clearly and specifically you define your dreams and goals. Determine exactly what you want, so you'll know it when you see it!

Have you ever gotten lost while driving? You had a map, but chose not to look at it? This kind of thinking ends up costing you valuable time and fuel and causes frustration. But if you know exactly where you're going, you won't get lost. You will take the road that gets you to your desired destination. Avoid being thrown off course by indecision and fear.

I hear students say, "I want a good job when I graduate." How would you define a good job? Is a good job determined by money, the location of the organization, the values of the organization, or the culture and environment of the organization? Is it determined by the benefits package or chance for career advancements?

We've all heard someone say, "I just want to be happy." What is happiness? What makes you happy now? What about your life pleases you? What steps must you take to remove the things that upset you? Imagine how happy you'll be once those obstacles are gone.

Brainstorming helps you put ideas on paper in a short amount of time. You only need a quiet place free of distractions (the calm,) paper and pen, and a stopwatch. Before you start brainstorming, think about an area of your life or career that you would like to improve. Are you ready to brainstorm? Get ready...now go!

Jermaine M. Davis

EMOTIONAL WISDOM

*"Emotional wisdom is the key ingredient to coping with life,
finding fulfillment, hope and the ability to know gratitude or grace."*

Ever hear yourself say something mean and wonder who was talking? Ever slam a door out of anger so hard the glass shakes, only to immediately hope no one witnessed (or heard) your loss of temper?

We all have those moments—even days! As human beings we all make mistakes. Sometimes we stop to consider our motivation and try to repair the damage we may have caused. We either move on from mistakes or hang onto them—blaming others or ourselves, stuck in shame (or anger) for a long time.

Unfortunately, many people (from children to adults) either forget or don't know how to learn from their mistakes. Many don't live in an environment which teaches, reinforces and models a better way to cope with the stress and emotions of life. Instead of learning from their poor judgment or difficulty managing their emotions, they react rashly. Many turn to harmful coping mechanisms, such as substance abuse and violence. What is lacking is emotional wisdom—the key ingredient to coping with life, finding fulfillment, hope, and the ability to know gratitude (or grace.)

You Can't Get One without the Other. You achieve emotional wisdom by consistently making healthy choices around the expression of your emotions. For example, instead of anger—you intentionally choose to be calm; instead of self-serving—you choose to be fair and patient; instead of complicating situations by analyzing too much—you choose the simple approach by trusting the outcome to God; instead of denial—you choose to be honest with yourself about other people's limitations, as well as, your own limitations; and instead of despair—you choose faith in a spiritual power and accept people as they are—flawed and all—as well as, yourself for doing the best you could do at the time.

Healthy choices are made through thought and a strong desire not to intentionally harm yourself or others. You recognize the unproductive outcome of retaliation and retribution. You understand the concept of self-control while accepting your inability to control other's thoughts, feelings and reactions—or what life may bring.

Are you born with emotional wisdom, or do you grow into it? My experiences working with youth have led me to the conclusion that very few children are learning emotional wisdom from their parents, schools and communities. Therefore, they resort to unhealthy or destructive ways to deal with emotions. Instead of learning about the values of respect, compassion, and spirituality, many children are being raised to value materialism and the acquisition of power. Their perspectives on life are rooted in: reaction versus responsiveness; vengefulness versus forgiveness; gossip rather than communication; fearfulness versus compassion and love; low self-esteem versus high self-worth; and negative behaviors versus positive expressions of emotion.

Achieving emotional wisdom begins with the ability (and desire) to identify what you are feeling and why. Becoming clear on whether it is anger or disappointment, for example, is useful in deciding whether you need to simply take some time to "cool down," make a new plan or get help in seeing your choices. Decisions made while angry are usually the wrong decisions and carry with them long-lasting negative feelings and unhappy consequences. We are not bad for feeling angry; it's what we do with our anger that really matters!

The next step to emotional wisdom is to recognize very few people make it alone—we all can use and grow from other people's help! Turn to those around you (or go find those) who are skilled at helping people understand their feelings and their reasons for what they feel. The more supportive such people are, the better! It's also important to recognize being supportive doesn't mean they will always agree with you. Often the people who have the greatest insight into our emotions (i.e. parents, teachers, friend's parents, ministers, youth group leaders, etc.) aren't going to make it easy for you by simply agreeing with you. Their compassion and concern for you will inspire them to be honest, genuine and helpful—sometimes sharing truths you don't really like to hear. Nevertheless, your life will be better if you seek their guidance and their emotional wisdom!

The last step in achieving emotional wisdom is to learn more constructive responses and coping mechanisms for the challenges and stressors of every day. How do you cope now? What do you do when you're about to lose it? How can prayer play a more significant role in your life? What healthy choices do you need to start putting on your list of helpful responses, and what behaviors, feelings and responses need to come off of your list?

One of the greatest stumbling blocks to emotional wisdom is the hiding, denying and suppressing of your feelings. These responses damage relationships or prevent them from happening at all. They make people distant, cold and full of self-pity. Instead of asking "Who can help me?" you ask, "Why me?" Instead of owning your unhealthy choices it becomes much easier and self-serving to blame everyone and everything for your problems or the consequences of poor choices.

It's All in Your Head. Brain scans studied by psychologists have shown the first place in your brain that gets activated when we make decisions is the emigdala. This is where you store emotional memories. This means that every decision we make starts with emotion. When parents do not show kindness towards their children or do not talk openly and with acceptance about emotion, children learn to protect themselves by hiding their real feelings. The children may feel wrong or bad for having feelings and teach themselves not to feel them (or become depressed or full of uncontrollable rage.) They learn a pattern of unhealthy choices in managing their emotions (i.e. blame, denial, dangerous escape mechanisms.) Such children become teens and adults who do not know their feelings, hide them, and risk losing touch with their true human potential. These children grow into adults unable to express themselves for fear of being hurt. Likely outcomes for adults who learned these unhealthy patterns as children include: alcoholism, drug addition, domestic violence, abusive relationships and divorce.

When parents, however, create home environments characterized by compassion, patience, kindness and courtesy, they foster emotional wisdom in their children. When a teacher responds with respect to a disenfranchised youth, he/she fosters emotional wisdom in that student. When a school counselor makes time in their excessively busy schedule to listen to the pain or hopelessness of a troubled child, he/she fosters emotional wisdom in a hurting human being. When a parent of a teenager asks, "What are you afraid of?" instead of yelling at the emerging adult, that parent fosters emotional wisdom in a confused young person.

Any time you stop to consider fear as the root of another's anger, denial, sense of worthlessness, hate, and jealousy you open the door to more useful emotional tools such as compassion, patience, kindness and courtesy! Any time you stop to pray or seek spiritual guidance before acting, you also open the door to being more helpful and understanding. Wherever you go for your Higher Power, go there often! Great emotional wisdom is found in prayer.

The Motivation to Move. Muscles don't like being pushed to do sit ups or stretched. Sitting is easier than standing. But, if you want to be more energetic, physically fit, resilient and strong, you get out there and move or exercise anyway! You know the cumulative benefit of daily movement and regular exercise. This knowledge motivates your actions. Emotional wisdom and the making of healthy choices also come from taking action when you don't feel like it! You can exercise your emotional wisdom even though you feel least like it—but, know you need the positive results!

How to Exercise Your Emotional Wisdom. I've developed a two step exercise for working through uncomfortable feelings, or handling confusing emotions, stress and conflict when it arises—before you say something you regret, slam a door too hard, or abuse substances as a way of escaping your pain. This exercise gives your brain an opportunity to express itself including the hidden tensions and emotional intensity. Unlike what you might have been taught growing up, it is good to have feelings and even better to be able to express them.

Keeping your feelings bottled up inside creates an internal pressure-cooker. In fact, the smallest of niggly-piggly fears held unexpressed in our minds will ping-pong about and create all kinds of unrelated and unrealistic judgments of ourselves and others! The process is simple.

Step One: On a piece of paper complete the following statement: I fear... (or Dear God, I fear...) Now let yourself write without stopping or editing your writing—no censuring! Express your anger, rage, sadness, insecurity, loss, and grief—whatever surfaces. Write it all down—don't give your thoughts free rent in your head! (A brain which is never allowed to express and release its fear becomes dysfunctional!)

Step Two: Now that you have more clarity of what you are feeling, reach out and contact someone you consider to be emotionally wise, supportive and understanding. Share honestly. This kind of confidante may be a teacher, therapist, psychologist, counselor, religious leader (i.e. pastor, priest or rabbi), friend, parent, member of a support group, or sibling. It always helps to reach out to someone who can relate to you, your feelings, and, perhaps, even your situation—and do so without judgment.

These two simple steps take considerable courage and a mustard seed of faith. Finding your emotional wisdom is believing things going wrong in your life have the potential to go right.

You deserve to be happy, joyous and free of emotional turmoil. Your life has meaning and you matter. As a human being, you are capable of enhanced emotional wisdom and all the blessings it brings to your life, and the world around you. I encourage you to seek emotional wisdom by acting with compassion, patience, kindness and courtesy; first and foremost towards yourself. You may then find an overflowing peace of mind and be truly ready to share more genuinely in relationship with others.

Susie Vanderlip

FOR A REASON

Sometimes I feel like I'm all by myself.
Sometimes I feel like there's nobody else.
But when I look deep inside.
And I stop trying to hide.
Maybe my life is out of focus for a reason.
Maybe my life is something I'm not supposed to understand.
Maybe my life is happening just the way you planned it.
Maybe my life is like the changing seasons, for a reason.
I've seen the sunset over the bayou of colors of red and blue.
I've seen the beauty of the mountain's view.
But I'm still searchin' for that place to call my own.
I'm still lookin' for that place I can call home.

Dr. Mari Ann Callais & Rhett Despeaux

HOW'S YOUR HEARING?

Do you find yourself frustrated after an exchange with your teenage son or daughter? Ever want to "beam back up to the ship" after getting scowls and disapproving looks by creatures you brought into this world, and are now considering taking out? Teenagers.

Since I began teaching, I've been particularly fascinated with the mind-set of teenagers. Like a mechanic, electrician, or detective, I've developed an obsession with figuring things out—especially when it comes to teenagers. My wife has already declared that our son will be my sole responsibility once he enters middle school.

While most parents pray (and teachers tremble) at the thought of trying to control (let alone teach) a hormone-driven teenager, I actually get excited about it. It's one of the many reasons I got into teaching. I like the challenge and want to be part of that teen's development.

I've learned over the years (by confession, rather than theory) about why these bundles-of-joy-turned-teenage-terrorists just won't listen to us. Oh, they're listening to someone; their friends, the media, entertainers, athletes, and others. They're just not listening to us—the guardians of their future. Why is that?

Regardless of how good we think we are as teachers, parents, authority figures, and interested parties, learning cannot take place without listening. We can't teach unless we can get and keep their attention. We have to be able to engage a student before we can educate a student. As parents, we need to connect with our teenage children before we can communicate with them.

Based on my observations and the evidence gathered as an educator, I believe we have room for improvement! Some might beg to differ despite a nearly 50% student dropout rate. I still say we have room for improvement in our ability to engage teenagers! What do you think? Is your relationship with the teenagers in your life where you want it to be?

In order to solve a problem, we must move beyond denial and admit a problem exists. I'll ask again: Why do our efforts to teach and influence teenagers and young adults fall short? Are you prepared to own the reason why teenagers might not be listening to you?

Here are five reasons teenagers don't listen to us—according to teenagers, themselves. Whether you have the honor of teaching teens, raising teens, or being in earshot of their cell phone conversations, what follows are relevant breakdowns in our dialogue with the generation charged with caring for us.

1. Because we don't (or won't) listen to them. It's important to understand this statement. If you've ever noticed, teenagers do some stupid things. If you ask your teenager, "Why did you do that?" After the standard initial response of "I don't know," the answer usually involves another guilty party. Some teenagers will blame a friend for their indiscretion or excuse their friend by saying, "We didn't see any harm in it."

The situation almost always involves another person; it's almost never a one-man job. It's amazing what teenagers can talk each other into trying, because it sounds like such a good idea at the time. So, what is the lesson? Teenagers will listen to anyone who listens to them. Despite how faulty (and dangerous) this kind of thinking can be, it is how they think. Ask yourself, "Do you really want your 13 or 16 year old seeking (and getting) advice from their peers with the same amount of life experience? Stop talking at them, and start listening to them.

2. Because they're questioning the source. Teachers (and parents) are pretty good at giving advice. It's in our "job" descriptions. Life has taught us many lessons, and as responsible adults, we feel obligated to pass our wisdom on to others (especially our own children). But as noble as our intentions are, there's one small problem: Teenagers don't believe half the stuff we're telling them. Why? Because we don't always model what we're teaching and preaching to them. Teenagers observe the inconsistency in what we tell them and what we do in our own lives. They "hear" our actions loudly and clearly. Do you say, "Treat your sister with respect" then slam the door on your spouse during an argument? Do you espouse the value of community service to your teenager then complain when it's your turn to serve coffee at "coffee hour"?

A simple rule of thumb I use with my students is to give them advice only if they've "been there and done that" themselves. If I haven't done it, and thus lack the experience and supporting evidence, I'll kindly point them in the direction of another teacher or adult who comes from where they speak. How can you effectively give advice on something you've never done yourself?

3. Because they're afraid of being judged or disappointing us. When it comes to teaching or raising teenagers, one of the toughest things to do is to learn when to keep our mouth shut. This is a lost art for those of us who enjoy our "air" time. I soon learned, however, that I wouldn't last a year if I didn't control my urge to fix, correct, solve, and resolve every student's problems. And here lies the dilemma—teachers are paid for knowing the answers! Is this why students isolate themselves and avoid us whenever they face serious problems?

NEVER be shocked by what a teenager tells you. I realized whenever a student told me something it was usually after it was done. And guess what? I couldn't do anything about it! It was already done. Regardless, I went into a long diatribe starting with any one of the following: How could you? What were you thinking? What should you have done?

No matter what I said after the fact, the outcome remained the same. Do these responses sound familiar?

Listen and withhold judgment. Stay calm. Never let them see you sweat. Only after you are asked to comment (which could take from a few minutes to a few days) should you say anything. And even then, ask questions about their feelings and thoughts—not just their actions. This approach has made all the difference over time. My students became much more willing to discuss serious matters when they believed I wasn't going to be "correcting" them or making them feel "wrong." Offer compassion and encouragement and be patient as you earn the trust of the teens in your world.

4. Because they're hurting. Most of my students, friends, and colleagues would consider me an empathetic listener. Learn this skill in different ways. I learned to "walk in someone else's shoes" as a result of growing up in a severely dysfunctional household. How have you learned to put yourself in the shoes of your teenager, or a room filled with them? What do you really know about their world, challenges and struggles—or the things that really bring them joy?

I am a product of a teenage mother, alcoholism, abuse, addiction, violence, criminal activity, an absent father, suicide attempts, depression, self-esteem issues, and poverty. The concept of a "hurting" teenager is very real to me. I was one. Not all of my students can understand my youth, yet it was mine for a reason. I have great understanding. I'm also not shy in sharing my story with students because people who've been hurt can offer healing to other hurting people.

People who are hurting and not healing can end up hurting themselves and others. Sometimes, the reason teenagers refuse to listen and learn, is that they are hurting in silence. I remember how strange it was that none of my high school teachers knew what I was going through at home. They didn't know because none of them had ever asked. Maybe it was because they didn't want to know. Was my story too painful for them? How were they supposed to treat me if they did know what I was going through? How should they ask?

Consider asking: How are you feeling today? If your teen or student says, "I'm fine," know that something isn't right. Listen to the alarm going off! In teenager language, "fine" may mean frustrated, insecure, neurotic and emotional. This is your cue to dig deeper. Sometimes it's helpful to assume that every teen you meet may be hurting or is getting ready to be hurt. Keep your antennae up! Listen for any signs saying, "This person needs to be heard." Proceed from there.

5. Because they're afraid of becoming us. This is a tough truth, but it needs to be said. Have you ever wondered why teenagers are drawn to poor role models? I've always been curious why so many of my students, for instance, seem so attracted to "gangsta" rappers, arrogant athletes, rebellious entertainers, womanizers, promiscuous women, and even lawbreakers! Is it because every one of these groups is presumably having more fun than we are?

How awful that we have taught our teenagers that if they do what we do, listen to what we say, and follow the path we recommend, they may end up at a destination called "boredom." They might just become us! If you don't believe me, ask yourself: "Would you want to grow up only to work a job you don't like, not get paid what you think you're worth, be financially strapped, end up in a lackluster marriage (or depressingly lonely life), always busy, and complaining most of the time?" Is this not what they see most adults (including their teachers) doing around them?

Would you want to listen to you? Consider the influence you have on those around you. Is it one of positive energy, fulfillment, joy and contentment? Live your life with passion, appreciation and enthusiasm. That's hard even for a teenager to ignore!

So, there's only one question left to ask: Are you worth listening to?

Enhanced understanding of why teenagers aren't listening to us is only the beginning. It's an important beginning, nevertheless. We can't take a stand against a problem until we first understand the problem. We can't help our youth mature, unless we mature in our empathy, communication skills and desire to connect (instead of write off) our teenagers.

I invite you to make a sincere commitment to improving your own life, by improving your ability to connect with a wonderful generation. Listen, instead of lecture. Sit, instead of solve. Empathize, instead of criticize. I guarantee you'll get through more often than you think.

So, how's your hearing?

Dr. Joe Martin

IT WILL ALL WORK OUT

I was invited by the local Rabbi to participate in the opening of a new center for Jewish college students in Buffalo. The program included prayers, tours, dances, and a brief service. Among the guests were leading supporters of the center, Jewish student leaders, and a few Jewish faculty members. These special guests were all seated in the front row for the service.

As part of the blessing of the new center, the Rabbi began by reading from the Torah, in Hebrew. After a few lines, he called his supporters, one by one to read more lines from the Torah, all in Hebrew. The student leaders then were called up, again, to each read a few lines, all in Hebrew.

In an instant, I saw what was coming. The Rabbi was calling all the special guests up to read, and I was next. I was going to be asked to read from the Torah and was expected to read some lines in Hebrew. This was not going to be pretty: This cradle Episcopalian knows no Hebrew.

The Rabbi finally nodded for me to come forward; it was my turn. I shook my head—No. The Rabbi nodded for me to come forward. I silently mouthed the words: "No, thank you" while shaking my head. The Rabbi smiled. I believed he got my message. He then looked at the gathered crowd and announced with a wide smile, "Our next reader will be University Vice President Dennis Black." I slowly rose to my feet and walked to the front of the crowd, very unsure about what would happen next and how I would ever survive!

As I went to the podium in fear, the Rabbi whispered to me, "Don't worry. It will work out." I took a deep breath, and looked at the right side page of the Torah, printed in Hebrew. Then I happened to look at the left side page of the book. It was printed in English. I smiled. I looked at the Rabbi. He smiled. And I read... in English.

Dr. Dennis Black

OLD POSTERS

D id you ever have the experience of opening a battered box in your basement and finding a treasure you had long forgotten? I recently opened such a well-worn box. Inside I found a tube of rolled up posters and immediately knew what they were and why I had saved them.

When I was an undergraduate at Florida State University many years ago, it was popular to adorn one's residence hall room with lots of posters. Many of my floor mates had posters of rock stars, or landscapes, or cartoon characters. I look back on those times and find it interesting that I had posters of several quotes that meant a lot to me then.

My three well-worn posters said:

"Not everything that is faced can be changed. But nothing can be changed until it is faced." - James Baldwin

"All of us are smarter than any of us."

"Nothing great was ever achieved without enthusiasm." - Benjamin Franklin

Somehow those three messages have been themes in my life. Somehow they emerged subconsciously in my 18 year old poster-buying mind and have been with me for the last 42 years. They shaped and reflect aspects of my philosophy of leadership.

These messages are apparent in the Relational Leadership Model that my friends Nance Lucas, Tim McMahon and I developed for our book *Exploring Leadership: For College Students Who Want to Make a Difference* (2007). That model encourages a relational approach to leadership that is purposeful, inclusive, empowering, ethical, and process-oriented. My belief in facing important issues, collaboration, commitment to shared goals, and passion and energy for things to which I commit myself all go back to those three well-worn treasures that I recently rediscovered in that basement box.

Look around you. How have you marked the space around you? What quote is at the end of your e-mail messages, what artifacts are on your bulletin board, what books are on your shelf, what music resonates, what web sites have you bookmarked? What themes do you see in your space that reflect the philosophies you bring to your own leadership? Make those messages transparent and perhaps mark your space with messages that others too can tell reflect your inner values, beliefs, and principles which guide how you try to be when you are with others.

Leadership is grounded in those beliefs and inspired by those values.

Dr. Susan R. Komives

THE JOURNEY

*"Most people search high and wide for the key to success.
If they only knew that the key to their dreams lies within."*

- George Washington Carver

Everything you have experienced in life so far has contributed to who you are today. Both the good and bad things in your life have come together to make you the person you've become.

The beautiful thing about life is that once you reflect upon your experiences, you come to see your challenges, joys, relationships and efforts from another perspective. There is great power within the realization that your challenges might just be blessings in disguise. And with this perspective, life takes on new meaning.

How can you slow down the fast pace of your life to reflect upon your daily miracles, character-building experiences, and precious moments? The first step is to make a commitment to yourself to contemplate your life purpose. The second step is to journal.

The process of writing your thoughts in a book, or journaling, is critically important for your personal and professional success. By reflecting upon your daily experiences, you begin to learn new life lessons. Journaling has taught me what truly matters in my life: loving relationships, trusting God, and enjoying priceless moments.

To illustrate the benefits of journaling, I will share a few journal pages written during a journey to Tanzania some years ago. As you read each entry, consider the many questions I ask, and then answer. Consider how I describe my experiences, record how I feel, and learn from my observations along the way.

Journal Entry—December 20: It's 1:15 PM and I'm flying from South Africa on Air Tanzania Airlines to Tanzania. I can't believe I'm about to do this. Questions are racing through my mind, *"What am I doing here?"* *"Will I make it?"* I hear someone say, "What you're about to experience will be unforgettable. The ten of you will attempt to climb Mount Kilimanjaro, the highest point on the African continent, and reach the summit in just five days on December 25th."

Am I ready? What do I really want?

My personal outcome for this trip is to strengthen my relationship with God in such a way that I will know with certainty that God is guiding my life. On Christmas Day, when I celebrate the birth of Jesus Christ, my desire is to have a glorious rebirth in my relationship with God.

It's been a long day. In forty-five minutes, I'll be at the hotel, ready for dinner and bed.

Personal Insight: In order to truly experience life to the fullest, you must have a clear desired outcome for each activity you do.

Journal Entry—December 21: As I wait for others to collect their gear, I must write about one of our three tour leaders—an incredible man named Msafiri. He's been up the mountain one hundred and forty six times. He is the tour captain.

There are twenty seven additional porters traveling with our group. They will carry the food, tents, and our big duffle bags with a change of clothes, toiletries, and equipment.

We have our backpacks containing water, snacks, medical pack, and smaller items like gloves, flashlights and sunscreen.

Someone told me earlier it would not rain today, so instead of packing my rain jacket, I have it in my big duffle bag which I will not see until the porters literally run ahead to set up the campsite.

I've been walking for the past five hours, the majority of which has been in a downpour. I'm soaking wet as I grab a moment under this tree.

Personal Insight: Always be prepared for the worst-case scenario to happen. It's better to have it and not need it, then to need it and not have it.

Evening has finally arrived. We set up the campsite and I'm teamed up to sleep in the same tent with a new friend, Joe, who snores. It's late and I can't sleep. I'm trying to "tune out" the noise, but am unsuccessful, so I write in my journal. I'm wondering how many times I need to say, "Joe, turn over!" before I can sleep. Here's another try...

Personal Insight: You must do what you need to do to achieve your desired results even if it means moving through conflict.

Journal Entry—December 22: It's a new day, almost 7:00 am and everyone appears to be up and having breakfast. I ask Msafiri, "Will it rain today?" He says, "No." Once again, I will put my trust in someone else and pack my rain jacket. Time to begin today's journey.

It's almost 9:00 am, and it's pouring. The rain is coming down and the wind has picked up. Not only am I wet, I am also freezing cold. Writing is becoming a challenge.

Personal Insight: You are ultimately responsible for the choices you make.

A quick break to catch our breath at last! We've been climbing rocks, crossing over streams and walking in mud. The scary part of the day came when we were crossing over a stream by walking on top of rocks. I lost my balance, soaked one foot, and almost fell into the stream. But being the graceful athlete (smile), I pulled it together and hopped my way to shore.

I'm finally by myself again, and taking a moment to recapture the last few hours. It's been a day of conversing with God, looking at beautiful sights, and reflecting on the meaning of life. Most of the group has walked ahead of me talking loudly. I just need some quiet time.

Personal Insight: Daily quiet time to reflect upon life, appreciate your experiences, and chart your future goals is keys to living a fulfilling life.

It's been one day walking in wet clothes with a strong wind blowing. I've managed to throw down a considerable amount of food at dinner. I'm ready for bed.

Journal Entry—December 23: I'm about to embark on a nine hour trek. Today I will pack my rain jacket and carry it with me. It's been a day already. As I write, I am still suffering from an apparent case of severe altitude sickness which began earlier in the day. People have been supporting me, but nothing is really helping. Writing is even draining my energy, but lifting my spirits. I am feeling really sick, and having a hard time breathing.

My mind is tripping, and I have this strange feeling of suffocation. I've never experienced this before. Just focus on breathing. Focus. I'm cold.

Personal Insight: You must appreciate what you have and not take anything for granted. When is the last time I thanked God for the blessing of good health? Isn't it interesting how most people appreciate something only when it's gone?

Journal Entry—December 24: Although I'm still suffering from altitude sickness, I'm going to try and eat some fruit at breakfast today. Others have noticed I'm still not feeling well. Just a moment ago, one of my companions said, "Marlon, you don't have to go to the top. Why don't you just relax and take care of your health?" I told him straight up, "You don't understand. My goal is to make it and I will make it." Focus.

Personal Insight: When there is no turning back, human beings will do EXTRA-ordinary things because they have to. When failure is not an option, you have no other choice but to succeed. It's amazing what you can do when you MUST. If you are casual about life, then you will likely become a casualty. I can do this.

It's now 5:30 PM. We are all totally exhausted. Msafiri just let us know we could rest for one hour before climbing another three hundred yards, and then return back to camp. He wants us to acclimatize to this altitude. Not something any of us wanted to hear.

It's almost 6:30 PM and only six of us are here.

Personal Insight: When things are going great, it's easy to smile. When things are going rough, you get to show your real strength by reaching deeper and focusing your thoughts on uplifting quotes, scriptures and affirmations. "As a man thinketh in his heart, so he is."

Christmas Eve is finally here. At dinner tonight, Msafiri told us to go to bed immediately because at midnight, we will be leaving in the dark to make our final climb to the summit of Mount Kilimanjaro. I'm still feeling nauseous. I want to sleep. I can do this.

Journal Entry—December 25: It's now 12:23 am. As I look around, everyone has their head flashlights, backpacks, and walking poles. It's time to move out. I'm mentally tired. My muscles hurt. I am spiritually strong. God is present. He will see me through the challenges ahead.

Wow! That was a close call. My climbing partner and I have taken a few tough falls on the ice so far, and Chris lost his light. As I went to help him, I slid out of control away from him. The guide was able to rescue Chris as I waited below in what felt like eternity.

Personal Insight: It always takes a team to produce incredible results.

The sun is rising making it easier to see at last. My watch reads 6:17 AM. Footprints appear in front of me. I will be able to follow these footprints up the mountain.

I just climbed my last rock and made it to the summit. I'm so excited. Wait...this is not the summit! We have about 150 more yards to go. I'm disappointed because in my mind, it's over. I need to go within for a moment and recite some scriptures for much needed inner strength.

Finally! I am at the summit by 10:23 AM. It is beautiful. Ice glaciers are all around me. Tears of joy roll down my face because I pushed myself, spiritually, mentally, and physically beyond anything that I have ever done before. This feels right. There is a sign which reads: Congratulations! You have successfully climbed

Mount Kilimanjaro, the highest peak in Africa, right to the summit—Uhuru Peak—5,895 meters. I will take pictures, and then head down the backside of the mountain.

Personal Insight: Success is found in the pursuit of your dreams and success definitely leaves footprints.

Fifteen hours have passed since my last entry. I'm starving. My legs are cramping. We are at a new campsite, but not home yet. I've been walking around like an old man, but am determined to finish what I started. I'm too tired to write much more. I just finished walking nineteen hours and four minutes. What a day.

Journal Entry—December 27: I am on a plane back to Johannesburg, South Africa. I plan on renting the first three Rocky movies and not getting out of bed until I've seen them all...three times! My body is sore, my spirit is soaring.

Personal Insight: It's up to each of us to do whatever is necessary to continue walking in our greatness. Live life to the fullest because tomorrow is not promised. Remember, the past is history and the future is a mystery.

There I am, my inner truths shared with you as a way of demonstrating the value in journaling. My thoughts, perspectives, attitudes, faith and action are revealed, along with what I learned on my journey about life, success, and determination. Throughout my writing, I notice my reliance on God and my relationship with Him. During every step of my journey, we kept our conversation going—through rain, sickness, miles and milestones. It was amazing.

By writing in a daily journal, you will appreciate the many miracles and blessings that happen every day in your life.

Questions for Journaling:

- What was good about today?

- What did I do today to move closer to fulfilling my <u>true</u> life mission?

- Who loves me and who do I love?

- What did I learn today?

- How has today added to the quality of my life?
- What am I grateful for in my life right now?
- What did I do today to illustrate my leadership skills?
- What am I most proud of in my life right now?
- What did I do today to contribute to someone else?

Marlon Smith

THE WORLD'S WORST WRESTLER

"I don't get your kid," said the father standing next to me with a smirk on his face. The smirk was meant to take the sting out of his comment, as if he was merely joking, but I understood. Kent and the other wrestling dads had been whispering for weeks, and Kent finally had the guts to say something to my face. Maybe, he thought, I would offer an explanation, an excuse, or a promise to never return to the gym.

My son was clearly the world's worst wrestler. Every practice, every match, my 9-year-old son was pinned in record time. Even when he wrestled boys who were years younger, he would end up on his back in seconds. Long and lanky, he looked like an injured bird, flapping his limbs in every direction. His face would turn red with effort, but he was dominated every night. You could see him trying to get free from his opponent and the inevitable loss. It never happened.

A week earlier, he lost to a girl. She was ten pounds lighter and a year younger. The other fathers' whispers turned into looks of pity. "Yeah, but he's having fun," I answered.

"That's what I don't get," Kent said. "I've never seen a kid have so much fun losing. It's weird." Again, with the smirk.

After each red-faced defeat, my son laughed and shook hands enthusiastically with the boy (or girl) who had just pinned him. Frequently, he was complimenting them on their awesome wrestling moves, and he always returned to the bleachers with a smile on his face. He was genuinely having a good time. It was freaking everyone out.

Kent's son hadn't lost to a girl yet, but the possibility loomed large. The kid was small for his age, and what he lacked in height and athletic ability, he made up for in nasty disposition. After each loss, Kent's son would storm to the sidelines, bark something angry at his father, call his opponent a "cheater," or declare the referee an "idiot" for failing to award him points for moves he imagined himself doing. Even the coach kept his distance, shouting a few encouraging words from 20 feet away, answered only with a scowl.

To his credit, Kent did everything he could to be a supportive father. He offered encouragement during the matches, gentle reminders of certain moves, and soothing words for his furious son after each match. This act was in vain, for Kent was clearly embarrassed by his son: the second worst wrestler in the world.

"Well, he's a fierce little competitor!" Kent would say, as his kid stormed off the mats in tears. "Fierce little crybaby," I'd say quietly under my breath. My son would giggle, and poke me in the ribs. "Be nice, Dad," he'd say. "He has issues."

In many ways, though, my son was the one with issues. Adopted only a year earlier, my little wrestler had been dealt a pretty tough hand having spent his earliest years cowering in fear of a violent, drug-abusing birth father. He spent months at a time in the squalor of a small trailer, under the inadequate care of his impoverished grandmother. Before he entered foster care at age six, he had never been shown how to brush his teeth. He had a few ragged toys, one pair of worn shoes, and a mouth full of cheap dental work the day I met him.

Things got better. He had been adopted by loving parents who provided him with a room of his own, clean clothes, and a school he loved. He had neighborhood friends and two dogs. Thriving in his stable environment, my boy laughed constantly and worked hard at his studies. He also talked incessantly about our first family vacation that first year.

"Does it bother you when you lose a wrestling match?" I asked him one night.

"Not really," he answered. "It's just fun to be able to do it."

The following weekend was the Big Brothers Tournament. Kids from wrestling programs throughout our metro area would be converging at a high school gym for a full day of matches. My son was incredibly excited. I marveled as dozens of small wrestlers in colorful singlets grappled in nine rings on the main floor of the gym. Parents shouted and cheered from the stands. Coaches "high-fived" winners and consoled the losers after each match.

In youth sports there are no winners and losers. For example, the best junior wrestlers—the ones who won all three matches—would go home with blue ribbons. Those who lost only one of their matches would leave with a red ribbon. Winning a single match earned a white ribbon. Even if a competitor lost all three matches, he would receive a yellow ribbon. Everyone got something. No one left empty-handed.

It was a relatively good day for Kent's son. When he lost two of his matches, he cried and pouted. When he finally won his final match, he erupted like he had won the Superbowl—all smiles and swagger. My son, the flapping bird, lost all three of his matches. In keeping with his spirit, he still laughed and made friends all day. At one point, he asked me to take a picture of him with the kid who beat him in his first match. During the lunch break, the two were playing in the high school's hallway, rough-housing and pretending to be their favorite professional wrestlers.

At the end of the day, the event organizers handed out ribbons. My son got a yellow ribbon, and grinned from ear to ear. Kent's son received the white ribbon, which he promptly threw in the trash. Kent shrugged, looking at me with both apology and pity. After all, his son had gotten white, and mine had only gotten yellow. "I don't get your kid," I said with a smirk.

"He's a competitor!" Kent shrugged, not getting the joke.

My son felt like he had been handed an Olympic medal. That afternoon, he pinned the yellow ribbon to his wall—the first ribbon or trophy he had ever received. Although he would go on to earn more in the months and years ahead, I was sure none would ever feel as important.

For Kent's son, anything short of a win was failure. Whether he won, lost, or "whatevered," it all meant victory to my son. He enjoyed just being there. He knew how to enjoy the moment and live the motto: "It's not whether you win or lose, it's how you play the game."

The world's worst wrestler taught me a great truth that season. The yellow ribbon I borrowed from his wall is still in my wallet as a gentle reminder of a powerful lesson: A victory on any given day depends on the grace with which you approach the challenge. Winning and losing is all relative when you consider the path that brought a man or woman, a boy or girl, to that moment. Simply being able to play the game—to be part of an activity, to go to college, to visit a special place, to be in a loving relationship—is victory enough.

By T.J. Sullivan

WHEN FAILING IS A BLESSING

Failing. A word that frightens most people. Whether it's failing a test in school, failing to perform well at work, failing to get a date with your secret crush, or failing—George Steinbrenner style, no one likes to fail!

And yet failing is part of succeeding. It's part of life. The more welcoming you are of failure, the more open you will be to the lessons it can teach you, and the more likely you will be to take risks. What kinds of risks? Those which challenge you to examine what you did right and what went wrong.

At thirty-nine years old, I became one of the nation's youngest African American college presidents. The average age of a college president is fifty. You might characterize my youthful days by the term, "over achiever." I worked hard and prioritized academic achievement. Have you ever tried to beat someone out for the top grade?

I graduated second in my high school class. I missed valedictorian by tenths of a point. I was forced to settle for salutatorian. Most high school students would have been thrilled. I was not. Second is not first. One of these days I know I will get over it!

My high school experience didn't end on a completely sour note. I was voted "Most Likely to Succeed." This is a much-coveted award which either represents the impending doom for the award-winner, or puts enough pressure on them to avoid failing at all costs. I take solace in having been elected student body president my senior year (after running and losing in 8th grade and as a freshmen and sophomore.) Why didn't I run my junior year? I needed a break from losing!

Academic achievement was always important to me. I knew that if I wanted to achieve my childhood dream of becoming a veterinarian, I'd have to have good grades, especially in the sciences. I remember at age twelve requesting and receiving brochures from every veterinary school in the country. I even knew each school's admissions requirements. I was looking ahead.

My science projects reflected my love of animals. From the 10th grade through my senior year, I studied rabbits and the effects of certain chemicals on gestation. We had rabbit hutches in our garage and bred rabbits for my projects. One of my favorite studies involved testing the effect of No-Doze on unborn bunnies. No-Doze contains caffeine and is used to keep tired people from sleeping. Once the bunnies were born, I weighed them and compared their weights against the control litter.

During the summer, I worked in veterinary hospitals. Experience would help me when it came time to apply to veterinary colleges. After high school graduation, I worked in a local pet store. I was focused and my plan was coming together. My academic record, combined with related work experience, would surely allow me to choose my college—including Ivy League schools. I was right.

Although I was admitted to Cornell University, this boy from "Hotlanta" settled on the University of Georgia. This was a comfortable distance from home, allowed me to become my own man, and it didn't snow! I quickly went into over-achiever mode and attempted to eliminate one year of requirements by overloading on required coursework, against my advisor's recommendations. My GPA suffered significantly, and I averaged 2.67 my first three semesters. I was in attack mode and enthusiastic about achieving my plan. My grades would go up.

My grades didn't go up. In fact, the pace was too quick. I wasn't in sync with the curriculum, and after a few exams I was looking at grades of "C" and "D." Work harder! Stay awake longer! You were voted "Most Likely to Succeed"! Many thoughts went through my mind, including the comforting reality that I just needed a "C" to pass. My solution? Commit to staying awake all night at least once a week to make sure I was learning the material. That worked.

Soon, I was staying awake three nights a week to learn the material. I felt like one of the rabbits I studied in my youthful science experiments. I was taking No-Doze as a regular part of my diet. Despite the health risks—stress and bad judgment—I continued on this path, barely hanging on to a "C" average. One failed exam and I was out of veterinary school and my dream would be over.

What do you do when you are supposed to be succeeding, but you are failing? Most of us go into denial, rationalize, or blame someone or something for our own lack of progress. Sometimes we downplay the significance of our dreams. Sometimes we simply give up or try to quit. I did all of these.

My destiny was at the mercy of my final exam grade in neuroanatomy. This was a devious course. Seventy-five percent of the grade was based on the final exam. You were given slides with slices of the brain and had to "guess" what the pins were indicating. If you knew what you were doing, you didn't actually "guess" because you knew. I guessed. I failed.

Of course, there was the make up exam. The thought of preparing again was overwhelming. In fact, it was just too hard. Shouldn't this have come easier to me if this was truly my destiny? Why was I pushing so hard for something that wasn't coming naturally to me? Is it possible that this isn't what I'm supposed to do with my life?

Instead of studying for the make up exam, I drove two and a half hours to a step show at West Georgia University. In the morning, I "guessed" my way through the exam again. I failed the exam. I failed the course. I failed veterinary college. I failed my dream. I failed me.

Why is failing a blessing?

Failing forces you to be honest. It makes you re-examine what you think you know about yourself. It makes you stronger, more humble and more mature. Failure enables you to see what success hides. With failure come the gifts of awareness, honesty and possibility. Failure doesn't mean you were wrong. It just means you weren't right.

One of the greatest outcomes of failure is the realization that there is a larger calling for you. Instead of letting your missed opportunities become a source of despair, allow your experiences to re-direct your efforts toward something more suitable. Don't be frightened by failure—worry more about succeeding! Ask for others' advice. Make a new plan, go back to school if you need, generate enthusiasm in a new chapter in your life, and set your sights on something more fitting your personality, skills, values and interests.

I did.

What have your failures taught you?

Dr. Walter Kimbrough

WHO I AM DEPENDS ON ME!

I am a human being.
I will fail, but I am not a failure.

There is good and bad in this world.
I will do bad things, but I am not bad.

There are right and wrong answers.
I will give wrong answers, but I am not wrong.

I am a collection of ideas, impressions and experiences.
I act upon this collection.
Every creature is a different collection.
We act differently. It's okay.

My failure may be your success.
My bad deed may be your good deed.
My wrong answer may be your right answer.
It's okay. We're different.

I am responsible for only one human being—me.
I know only one collection—my own.
Who I am depends on me!

Patty Hendrickson

Contributing Authors

Rick Barnes, M.A.: After a sixteen year career in student affairs administration Rick became a full time speaker specializing in leadership and alcohol responsibility. Rick is a speaker, consultant, trainer and personal coach, providing *educational programs that make a difference!* He is the past president of the Association of Fraternity Advisors and Chair of the AFA Foundation, and currently serves on the Board of Directors of the North-American Interfraternity Conference. He is a member of FarmHouse Fraternity where he served as International Vice President.
Contact Information: 817.788.5019
    Internet: www.rickbarnespresents.com

Dennis Black, JD: Currently serves as Vice President for Student Affairs at the University at Buffalo (UB), providing leadership and vision to a division serving 25,000 students. Engaged in the university and community, he an adjunct assistant professor in the Graduate School of Education and serves as a trustee of a local college. As an administrator, instructor, and attorney, Dr. Black speaks, writes, and consults on student service and legal concerns for educational organizations and institutions. He is Editor of *Perspective: The Campus Legal Monthly* newsletter, with a national circulation of over 1,500 colleges and universities. Dr. Black is an active member of the National Association of Student Personnel Administrators (NASPA) and serves on the Board's of the National Academy for Leadership and Executive Effectiveness and the NASPA Journal.
Contact Information: 716.645.2982, dblack@buffalo.edu
Charity: Hospice (www.palliativecare.org/foundation/)

Mari Ann Callais, Ph.D: Specializes in fraternity and sorority rituals and consults with universities and fraternities and sororities throughout the country. She serves as the Theme Housing Specialist for Capstone Development and is serving in her third term as National President of her sorority: Theta Phi Alpha Fraternity. Mari Ann currently serves on Editorial Board and is a member of the Peer Review Panel for *Oracle: the Research Journal for the Association of Fraternity Advisors*. Mari Ann is a former assistant professor and Student Affairs Program Coordinator at Mississippi State University. She released a CD of original music entitled, *Out of Focus*.

Contact Information: mac@marianncallais.com,
    www.marianncallais.com
Charity: Camp Friendship

David Coleman, M.A.: Known worldwide as "The Dating Doctor"™ and "America's Real-Life Hitch!" He is the recipient of national speaker of the year honors by *Campus Activities Magazine* and the *National Association for Campus Activities* and has contributed to *Glamour, Cosmopolitan, Women's World, Celebrity Living, Us, ESPN The Magazine, The New York Times* and *The USA Today* among many others and has been featured on *CNN* and *Access Hollywood*. His topics include: human relationships, leadership and the development of character.

Contact Information: 1.866.DateSmart, www.DatingDoctor.com
    or www.MySpace.com/DatingDoctorPage

Maura Cullen, Ed.D: As a full time educational consultant and speaker since 1987, Maura provides training programs and keynote addresses throughout the United States, Canada and Australia. She received her doctorate at the University of Massachusetts – Amherst in Social Justice and Diversity Education and is a founding member of the Social Justice Training Institute. Also a certified Firewalking Instructor, her real passions include her family, her dogs and the outdoors.

Contact Information: www.MauraCullen.com

Doug Cureton, M.A.: Founder and senior consultant for CreativiTEAM Inc., a Fort Lauderdale based company offering personalized leadership and diversity training programs to colleges and universities, major Fortune 500 corporations, community organizations and law enforcement agencies. He serves on the Facilitator Staff of the FutureWork Institute and as a Senior Training Consultant for the Anti-Defamation League A World of Difference Institute. He is co-author of *Let Your Leadership Speak: How to Lead and Be Heard* and owner of *What's The Scoop?* - a gelateria in Wilton Manors, Florida.

Contact Information: 954.522.5883, www.CreativiTEAM.com

Charity: UNICEF (www.unicef.org)

Jermaine M. Davis, M.A., M.Ed: "The Inspirational Teacher" began his professional career in corporate America before becoming a college professor of Communication Studies at Century College in Minnesota where he was awarded the College Instructor of the Year Award. Jermaine beat the odds and made it out of the inner city of Chicago's housing projects and with the consistent studying of success principles, Jermaine became the founder and president of Seminars & Workshops, Inc., and Snack Attack Vending of Minnesota. Jermaine is also the author of: *Get Up Off Your Butt & Do It NOW, Leading with Greatness, Be Diversity Competent, and You Don't Have to Sell Out to Stand Out.* Jermaine holds a MA in both Speech Communication and Education. Jermaine's topics include: Overcoming Obstacles, Communication, Diversity, Leadership, Motivation, Team Building, and Women's Leadership.

Contact Information: 651.487.7576, www.jermainedavis.com, jermaine@jermainedavis.com

Charity: The Dorothy Baughman and Carolyn "**Charmaine**" Davis Scholarship Fund

Nancy Hunter Denney, M.A.: After spending twelve years in higher education student affairs, Nancy founded Potential Leadership Training and Lectures in 1993 where she specializes in inspiring those who make a difference in other's lives through her high energy style of speaking, original material, humor and spiritual calling. Her audiences include non-profit helping organizations, woman's leadership events, health care associations, leadership conferences, and institutions of higher education. In addition to numerous inspirational sayings, videos and products, she is the author of: *Zing! Your Life and Leadership: 21 Insights on Maximizing Your Influence*, *Let Your Leadership Speak,* and *Life by Design.* Nancy has national keynote appearances with Suze Orman, Dr. Phil, Soledad O'Brien, Dana Reeves—to name a few. In 2006, Nancy founded Zing! Leadership Development Systems, LLC, a company providing curriculum development, leadership training resources and specialized ocean front professional development retreats.

Contact Information: 888.566.7536, www.nancyhunterdenney.com
    or www.zingleadership.com
Charity: Advent House (homeless shelter) – Providence, RI

Laura De Veau, M.A.: As a former stand-up comedian, Laura has a great deal of experience behind a microphone. As a veteran student affairs administrator, she has used the often-humbling experience on stage as a driving point in her on-target presentations. Laura prides herself on making each presentation something special for her clients by combining humor with a "here's the point" style of presenting. Her expertise is in the areas of Residence Life, Leadership and Student Engagement. A graduate of Boston University's School of Education and College of Communication, Laura holds a M.A. in Higher Education Administration. She currently serves as the past-president of the Massachusetts Association for Women in Education, is on the American Council of Educators Massachusetts Office of Women in Higher Education Massachusetts board, and is a committed member of the National Association of Student Personnel Administrators, who awarded her it's 2006 Outstanding Mid-level professional award. Laura holds the position of Assistant Director for Student and Staff Development at Boston University's Office of Residence Life.

Contact Information: www.deveautrain.com
Charity: Wide Horizons for Children (www.whfc.org)

Mike Domitrz: Founder of The Date Safe Project, an organization dedicated to producing powerful programs and compelling materials for youth on consent, healthy dating, and sexual assault awareness. After his sister was sexually assaulted in 1989, Mike began speaking in schools presenting his one-person show titled "Can I Kiss You?" Known for his hilarious sense of humor combined with hard-hitting emotion, he shares how "Asking First" and "Opening the Door" makes all the difference. He is the author of the critically-acclaimed book *May I Kiss You?* and the editor of *Voices of Courage.*
Contact Information: 800.329.9390, www.canikissyou.com or
   www.thedatesafeproject.org
Charity: R.A.I.N.N. (Rape, Abuse, & Incest National Network)

Lori Hart Ebert, Ph.D: Brings 10 years experience speaking throughout higher education specializing in relationships, alcohol, and Greek life. Currently, Dr. Ebert serves as the Director of Alcohol Education for Pi Kappa Phi Fraternity, represents Alpha Omicron Pi at the National Panhellenic Conference and is a member of the Peer Review Panel Member for *Oracle: the Research Journal for the Association of Fraternity Advisors.* On a volunteer level, she served as a Mentor for the National Conference on Ethics in America at West Point Military Academy and Chairman of the Alcohol and Recruitment Committee for the North American Interfraternity Conference.
Contact Information: 404.816.0111, ebert@campuspeak.com,
   www.campuspeak.com/speakers/hart-ebert/
Charity: Push America: National Philanthropy of Pi Kappa Phi
   Fraternity

Ed Gerety, CSP: Ed is a keynote speaker and leadership trainer for students, parents, and those who work with youth. His presentations focus on respect, responsibility, goal-setting, and communication. An expert on student leadership, Ed has spoken to audiences in all 50 states, Canada, and Europe reaching over one million people and counting. He is the author of *Combinations: Opening the Door to Student Leadership* and a contributing author of three books in the popular *Teen Power* series with over 250,000 copies in print. The National Speakers Association awarded Ed their highest earned designation and international measure of platform skill, Certified Speaking Professional (CSP), an honor held by less than 10% of the over 4000 members who belong to the International Federation of Professional Speakers. Ed graduated with his BA in Communications from The University of New Hampshire and has completed the Boston Marathon three times.

Contact Information: 800.207.2580, www.EdGerety.com

Charity: United We Stand for Jason (Huntington's Disease)

Joel Goldman: Since 1992, Joel has spoken to college and high school students on the subjects of alcohol, sex, and HIV and is a consultant to non-profits helping them secure and media train celebrity spokespeople for their causes. He has worked with St. Jude Children's Research Hospital, Elizabeth Glaser Pediatric AIDS Foundation, America's Second Harvest, and The Alliance for Children's Rights. Joel serves on the Board of Directors of Camp Heartland—a national organization that provides year-round support for children infected and affected by AIDS. A former International President of his Fraternity, Sigma Alpha Mu, Joel now serves as the National Philanthropy Chairman

Contact Information: joel@campuspeak.com.

Charity: Camp Heartland (www.campheartland.org)

Maureen Hartford, Ed.D: Named president of Meredith College in February 1999. She is the first female president of Meredith, the largest private college for women in the Southeast. She serves on numerous boards, including the Marine Corps University Board, the Greater Raleigh Chamber of Commerce Board of Directors, and serves as chair of the national LeaderShape governing board. She was named to the Board of Directors for the North Carolina Citizens for Business and Industry. Hartford holds bachelors and master's degrees from the University of North Carolina in Chapel Hill. Her doctorate in higher education administration is from the University of Arkansas.

Patty Hendrickson, CSP: Patty works with organizations that want to grow leaders and with people who want more out of life. Patty's high-energy and interactive programs gently encourage audience members to examine themselves and take action. Since 1987 Patty has been sharing her enthusiastic message throughout the world. She has a Masters of Business Administration and is the author of many books. In 2000, Patty received the highest earned designation of Certified Speaking Professional from the National Speakers Association – an honor given to less than 600 speakers in the world. Her most popular topics are leadership, emerging leaders and motivation. Patty's energy inspires so her message sticks!

Contact Information: 800.557.2889, Patty@pattyhendrickson.com

Charity: The Smile Train (www.smiletrain.org)

Patti Holmes: President of Holmes Training and Development, an Oxford, Ohio company founded in 1988. She has delivered over 1,000 presentations to audiences as diverse as Proctor and Gamble, The Home Shopping Network, Fidelity Investments, The US Army in Europe, General Electric and over 100 colleges and universities. She provides dynamic keynote addresses, educational workshops and leadership coaching to increase personal capacity and develop competencies for great productivity and organizational excellence.   From Frankfort, Kentucky to Frankfort, Germany she has spoken to groups in 41 states, in addition to Canada, Mexico, Bahamas, Europe, and Russia. She is the author of the book, *"What Do Followers Expect of Leaders?"* published in 2002, and now in its second edition. Prior to founding her company in 1988, Patti served as both an administrator in Student Affairs and faculty member at three colleges and universities: The University of Dayton, North Harris Community College in Houston, Texas, and Miami University in Oxford, Ohio. Consistently engaging, results driven, down right fun *and serious*, Patti is known to resonate with focus and passion. She is most proud of her three children Erin, Ryan and Mattie and believes this is where she gets her richest stories and best material.

Contact Information: 513.523.1394, www.pattiholmes.com,

pholmes@pattiholmes.com
Charity: Bethany House Services, Cincinnati, Ohio

Will Keim, Ph.D: Considered "the dean" of inspirational speakers in higher education having spoken to over two million students from 2000 campuses, Dr. Keim speaks on character driven decision making, values and ethics, actualizing peak performance, substance abuse, and leadership. He is the author of twelve books including: *The Education of Character: Lessons for Beginners, Spirit Journey, Life after College, The Truth about College, and the Tao of Christ* and is the contributing author to *Chicken Soup for the College Soul*. Dr. Keim is an NCAA Recognized Speaker, Paul Harris Fellow (awarded by Rotary International) and was selected at the Outstanding Professor of The Year at Oregon State University. He holds as his greatest "accomplishments" his four children Christa, Samantha, J.J., and Hannah and his 26 year marriage to Donna. He serves as the Intercollegiate Chaplain for the Christian Church (Disciples of Christ) and International Chaplain for his fraternity, Delta Upsilon International Fraternity. Dr. Keim's newest endeavor is a partnership with Educational Options, Inc., the US Chamber of Commerce Outstanding Small Business of The Year Recipient, which is releasing a number of On-Line E Courses that will make Dr. Keim's message available around the world, 24/7 and provide instant access to information that encourages people to Live Lives That Matter. Will Keim holds a Ph.D. in Education with an emphasis in College Student Services Administration from the Oregon State University.
Contact Information: 800.848.3897, www.willkeim.com or
www.edoptions.com, willkeim@att.net
Charity: Children's Miracle Network

Walter Kimbrough, Ph.D: At 37 years of age became the 12th president of Philander Smith College in Little Rock, Arkansas and the first college president from the hip-hop generation and one of the youngest college presidents in the nation. He is the author of *Black Greek 101: The Culture, Customs and Challenges*

of Black Fraternities and Sororities. Considered a national expert on historically Black fraternities and sororities, Dr. Kimbrough has appeared in the Washington Post and The Chronicle of Higher Education and on NPR's "Talk of the Nation." He is a member of the board of directors for the Greater Little Rock Chamber of Commerce, as well as the Heart of Arkansas United Way. Dr. Kimbrough earned a BS from the University of Georgia (1989), MS in College Student Personnel Services (1991), and a Ph.D in Higher Education from Georgia State University.
Contact Information: www.philander.edu
Charity: United Negro College Fund

Susan R. Komives, Ed.D: Serves as a senior scholar at the James MacGregor Burns Academy of Leadership and an associate professor at the University of Maryland. An expert on leadership development in young adults, Komives has served as vice president for student development at the University of Tampa, vice president and dean of student life at Stephens College in Columbia, Missouri, and associate dean of students at Denison University in Granville, Ohio. She is a co-author of *Exploring Leadership: for College Students Who Want to Make a Difference* and the fourth edition of *Student Services: a Handbook for the Profession* and was co-founder of the National Clearinghouse for Leadership Programs.
Contact Information: www.education.umd.edu/edcp/csp

Jud Laipply, M.A.: Creator and dancer of one of the Internets most popular videos of all time "The Evolution of Dance" Judson has been seen on a wide range of TV shows, featured in numerous media outlets, and has established himself as an online presence. Working full time as a professional speaker, Judson weaves humor and content to create a one of a kind experience. "The Evolution of Dance" caps his high energy performance and is loved by audiences of all ages. He newest company, Let's Dance Media, is helping to change the Internet with the launch of LiveLoud.tv an online network dedicated to helping people across the globe.
Contact: www.judson.tv
Charity: Bacchus and Gamma National Peer Education Network

Marilyn Levin, MSW, CAPSW: Uses her talents as a trainer and speaker to ignite the passion, power and possibility that lives within each of us! Marilyn's participants rave about her ability to move groups past where they thought they could go, leaving them thoroughly satisfied and empowered to transform their lives. Marilyn is an award winning activist, educator and athlete with a broad range of experience in social work, youth work, experiential education and social justice/transformation work.
Contact Information: www.marilynlevin.com
Charity: The Pachamama Alliance (www.pachamama.org)

Joe Martin, Ed.D: At the age of 24, Dr. Martin became the youngest tenured-earning faculty member ever hired to teach at an accredited state university in Florida, and was also the youngest to ever be nominated for the Distinguished Teacher's Award (twice) at his academic institution. Through his creation of RealWorldUniversity.com, Dr. Martin he helps more than 110,000 students per month meet the academic, personal, and professional challenges of college and life; and through his award-winning web site www.NewTeacherSuccess.com, he assists, supports, and sustains the retention and professional development of America's teachers.   Dr. Martin is the current host of the "Good Teachers" radio talk show on WTAL 1450-AM in Tallahassee, Florida, and is the author of seven books, including: "Tricks of the Grade," "Gifts and Handkerchiefs," "Stop Parenting & Start Coaching," and "Let Your Leadership Speak." He also serves as a guest columnist for three national publications: *Student Leader Magazine, The Black Collegian,* and *The Teachers Gazette.*
Contact Information: 888.576.2377, www.professormartin.com
Charity: The Character Center for Kids in Tallahassee, Florida (www.character4kids.com)

Delatorro L. McNeal, II: As the CEO and President of Delatorro Worldwide Empowerment, Delatorro operates three blossoming corporations. He was most recently named "One of the Top Four Best Campus Speakers" of 2004 & 2005. In addition, The Tampa

Bay Business Journal recently named Delatorro as "One of the Top 30 Under 30" an award of distinction given to the top thirty outstanding business leaders in the Tampa/St. Pete Metropolis. Additionally, Delatorro was a finalist for the 2006 Young Minority Business Person of the Year. He is the author of four books including: *Robbing The Grave of Its Greatness, and The Rules of the Game.* As a successful entrepreneur, Delatorro recently launched his own Motivational Clothing line called, EMPOWEAR (pronounced M-pow-wear), "The Gear that Ignites Greatness!" and operates an online shopping mall at www.BuyEmpowear.com. Corporations, colleges, professional associations, churches, conferences, school systems, and civic organizations call on Delatorro to deliver over 100 power-packed presentations each year. Affectionately known as "The Greatness Guy," Delatorro takes audiences by storm with his powerful, practical, and paradigm-shifting keynotes and seminars centered on his mantra that, "Goodness is free, but Greatness will cost you! The question is, are you ready to pay the price?"
Contact Information: 866.472.8637, www.DelMcNeal.com or
www.BuyEmpower.com
Charity: United Negro College Fund

Micheal Miller, M.A.: Michael is "the happiest person he knows!" That said—Michael has a unique take on life given his experiences growing up in The Bronx, New York City. Michael finds being direct and honest easier than most—allowing him to mix humor and passion in a way that makes him memorable and motivational! An intense and true living defines his every move—and will inspire the same in you. As a leadership consultant and featured presenter you'll find Michael's bold and engaging approach useful in improving your organization and institution. Currently he spends around 200 nights a year on the road helping organizations and individuals get what they want out of their time and their lives. Look for more on Michael as his website www.reallymotivated.com comes on line early this year.
Contact Information: 320.259.8222, www.hit4you.com or www. reallymotivated.com

Elaine Penn, M.Ed.: A nationally recognized motivational speaker and trainer, Elaine specializes in leadership, personal success, wellness and diversity. Prior to becoming a full time speaker, she worked in higher education for 14 years in a variety of positions, including Director of Special Projects; Chief Fund Raiser and executive producer of five television documentaries about environmental and social issues; Director of Campus Recreation and Assistant Volleyball Coach. An outstanding college athlete, Elaine was inducted into the Greensboro College Sports Hall of Fame in 1996. Also a singer-songwriter, Elaine incorporates inspiring music into her programs.
Contact Information: elaine@elainepenn.com, www.elainepenn.com
Charity: Humane Society

Kristin Skarie, M.S.Ed.: Founder and President of Teamworks, a consulting company committed to building great leaders and teams, Kristen brings 20 years of experience to her extensive development work with colleges, corporations and community organizations. She and her team believe; leadership is rooted in the cultivation of knowledge, skills and competencies to create shared vision, maintain open communication and promote regular opportunities for fun at work. Kristen is highly involved with the American College Personnel Association and is a facilitator with LeaderShape, Kiwanis International, the Girl Scouts and the American Red Cross. Her degrees are from the University of Wisconsin and Indiana University. Kristin's faith, gratitude for family and friends and sense of humor keep her grounded.
Contact Information: 585.425.1506, kskarie@betterteams.com,
    www.betterteams.com
Charity: Jumpstart (literacy organization) (www.jstart.org)

Lance "Claysmile" Smith: Founder of Dependent Branch Entertainment, Lance performs exhilarating one-person motivational stage plays that have been loosely inspired by his life experiences. He is an icon of hope for many youth with his compelling stories of resisting peer pressure, overcoming challenges, pursuing academic

excellence, and making a difference in our world.
Contact Information: 301.325.2379, www.claysmile.com
Charity: American Red Cross

Marlon Smith, M.A.: Before founding Success By Choice, Inc.—a company created with the mission of empowering our global society by helping individuals realize their true potential - in 1992, Marlon worked for IBM and Hewlett-Packard as a systems engineer. Known as the "High-Tech Motivator," Marlon has given keynote presentations in 45 states and 13 countries. In South Africa, he produced the "Motivational Mondays" television series, as well as, the national "Success is Your Choice" radio program. Marlon is the co-producer of the Real Men Talking multimedia stage production which is currently touring the US helping young people and families maximize their true potential. He is the author of numerous books including: *Living with Purpose... 40 Days to Empowering You and Your Family* (NEWLY RELEASED), *What's Up?- A Solution Guide For Today's Young People, Voices of Inspiration* and is a contributing author to the best selling book, *A Second Helping of Chicken Soup For The Soul.*
Contact Information: 800.321.2464, www.successbychoice.com
     or www.realmentalking.com
Charity: New Faith Outreach Ministry

Clay Stauffer: In addition to serving as the Associate Minister for Evangelism, New Members, and Young Adults at Lindenwood, Rev. Stauffer speaks to college students, teachers and organizations on: the power of leadership, restoring faith in the clergy, ethics and values, happiness and living a simple life. Clay is dedicated to inner city ministry and also serves as Chaplain for the Phoenix Club of Memphis, an organization that raises money for Memphis' Boys and Girls Club. He received his Master of Divinity degree from Princeton Theological Seminary in 2005.
Contact Information: 901.458.8506, clay.stauffer@lindenwood.net
Charity: The ministry of his local congregation.

Karin Stende, M.S.: With a widely diverse background, Karin Malkowski Stende offers trainings on conflict management, communication, and mediation to college students and professionals in education. She is a contributing editor to: *College Success Secrets: What They Don't Teach You in the Classroom.* She is a registered mediator practicing in the Georgia court system, and is a meeting facilitator, a certified ombudsman, and conflict management consultant. Karen has coached numerous state speech champions and taught at-risk students.

Contact Information: 866.2STENDE [278.3633],

karin@StendeInspirations.com, www.stendeinspirations.com

Charity: Doctors Without Borders (www.doctorswithoutborders.org)

Troy Stende: A former NCAA Division One gymnast, Troy actively strives to inspire and teach leadership to college students through Stende Inspirations and a high energy style of presenting. He has received three awards for his ability to connect with his audiences from the Association for the Promotion of Campus Activities. Troy is a contributing editor to: *College Success Secrets: What They Don't Teach You in the Classroom.* He has appeared on National Public Radio, and was featured in USA Today.

Contact Information: 866.2STENDE [278.3633],

www.stendeinspirations.com, troy@troystende.com

Charity: America's Second Harvest, Nations Food Bank Network (www.SecondHarvest.org)

T.J. Sullivan: Co-founded CAMPUSPEAK, a company dedicated to providing quality educational speakers and programs to college campuses, conferences and organizations, and since 1989 has earned a positive reputation as a speaker on tough issue facing college students. As a professional speaker, T.J. has appeared before one million students on more than 1000 campuses nationwide. He has won top national awards from the Association of Fraternity Advisors, the North-American Interfraternity Conference, and his own fraternity, Pi Kappa Phi.

Contact Information: 303.745.5545, sullivan@campuspeak.com

Charity: Adoption Exchange (promotes the adoption of children currently in foster care) (www.adoptex.org)

Gary Tuerack: Nationally recognized inspirational speaker and founder of the National Society of Leadership and Success (Sigma Alpha Pi) - a unique organization with the sole purpose of creating long-term positive change in college students' lives. The society focuses on providing the tools, support, skills and motivation students need to identify and achieve their aspirations. With a nationwide network of chapters and over 20,000 members, the organization empowers personal growth through training, team building, personal accountability, and exposure to many nationally known leadership and motivational speakers and authors.
Contact Information: 800.601.6248, www.societyofsuccess.com

Johnnie Tuitel: Founded *Alternatives in Motion*, a non-profit organization that purchases wheelchairs for people needing financial help with their mobility and is a leading speaker for youth and higher education, corporations, and sports teams on the topic of *Handicapitalism*^{SM}. Johnnie is the author of six children's books in the *Gun Lake Adventure Series* (The unique hero is a boy in a wheelchair). He is the five time recipient of the *State of Michigan United Way* "Speaker of the Year" award and in 1997; Johnnie received the WOOD TV8 Unsung Hero's Award for community service from President Gerald R. Ford. In 2003, he was honored as a distinguished alumni of Hope College in Holland, MI. In 2005, The Rotary Foundation named Johnnie a Paul Harris Fellow. He lives with his wife Deb, and three boys in Grand Rapids, MI.
Contact Information: 888.302.7463, www.johnnietuitel.com
Charity: Alternatives in Motion (www.alternativesinmotion.org)

Susie Vanderlip, CSP: Creator and performer of LEGACY OF HOPE, Susie is best known as "the Dancer" or as "Julio the gangbanger"—one of eight distinct characters in her original one-woman theatrical program. Since 1991, she has been on tour dramatically addressing such issues as: alcohol and drug abuse, irresponsible sexuality, gangs, violence, self-harm, depression and other destructive choices. Her audiences include middle schools, high schools, colleges, faculty development, parent awareness, mental health professional education, women's events and recovery conferences. Susie is an approved speaker by the NCAA for collegiate athletic alcohol and drug education, a certified teacher of Actualism Meditation and coach to youth and families of alcoholics/addicts over 24 years old. She consultants on emotional wisdom, stress management and family dynamics and is the author of *52 Ways to Protect Your Teen – Guiding Teens to Good Choices and Success.* Her professional dance experiences include serving as a dance professor at Coastline Community College for 12 years, and as executive director/choreographer/dancer of a regional dance company for 25 years.

Contact Information: 800.707.1977, www.legacyofhope.com or www.WaystoProtect.com

Charity: World Vision Home Church – Irvine United Congregational Church, 4915 Alton Parkway, Irvine, CA 92604.

Vernon Wall, M.A.: Brings twenty plus years of professional experience in higher education to his speaking and training in the areas of oppression, social justice and leadership styles. Vernon has degrees from North Carolina State University and Indiana University and has worked in student affairs positions at UNC – Charlotte, UNC – Chapel Hill, University of Georgia and Iowa State University. He has experience in residence life, new student orientation, Greek life, student activities international education and leadership programs. In the spring of 1998, Vernon was a member of the student life staff with the Semester at Sea program accompanying 600 students on a voyage around the world. He is also one of the founding faculty members of the Social Justice Training Institute. Vernon has won several awards for his contributions to the quality of student life and has co-edited two books and written several articles on issues of inclusion on today's college campus.

His award winning programs and presentations have been seen by thousands of students, faculty and staff on campuses around the country and have been described as: "a learning experience with a touch of wildness."

Contact Information: www.vernonwall.org

Charity: The Boybutante AIDS Foundation (www.boybutante.org)

Jamie Washington, Ph.D: President and Founder of the Washington Consulting Group, a multicultural organizational development firm out of Baltimore. His topics include: diversity, leadership, spirituality, organizational change and community development issues. Dr. Washington has served as an educator, speaker and administrator in higher education for over 20 years before becoming a full time consultant and currently is a faculty member of the Social Justice Training Institute. He recently became on ordained minister and serves as an Associate Minister at Unity Fellowship Church of Baltimore where he shares his musical and inspirational talents. Dr. Washington received his Master of Divinity from Howard University School of Divinity in May of 2004.

Contact Information: www.washingtonconsultinggroup.net

Charity: United Negro College Fund

Curtis Zimmerman: Recipient of the prestigious 2005 National Leadership Award from United States Congressman Tom Reynolds, Curtis Zimmerman educates people to be character driven leaders who make ethical decisions, handle conflict creatively and take responsibility for their actions. A native of Los Angeles, California, Curtis incorporates the skills he gained from over twenty years in the entertainment business into his powerful and far-reaching programs, cleverly balancing the connection between education and entertainment. Curtis is the author of *I believe...what do you believe?*, co-author of *Keys to Success in College and Life*, and a contributing author to *Pillars of Success*. Curtis is a member of the National Speakers Association and an NCAA certified speaker. His other awards include: Universal Studios Entertainer of the Year, and a nomination by the Association for the Promotion of Campus Activities for National Speaker of the Year!

Contact Information: 513.229.3626, www.curtiszimmerman.com
Charity: Gift of Sight

Bibliographical References

Coelho, Paulo. The Alchemist: A Fable About Following Your Dream. San Francisco: Harper San Francisco, 1995.

Dickens, Charles. A Tale of Two Cities. New York: Signet Classic/ Penguin Books USA, 1980.

Frankl, Viktor E. Man's Search for Meaning. New York: Simon & Schuster Inc, 1984.

Fulghum, Robert.   All I Really Need to Know I Learned in Kindergarten: Uncommon Thoughts on Common Things. New York: Random House, 1988.

Osbon, Diane. Reflections on the Art of Living: A Joseph Campbell Companion. New York: Harper Collins Publishers, 1991.

Ruiz, Don M. The Four Agreements: A Practical Guide to Personal Freedom.   San Rafael, California: Amber-Allen Publishing, 1997.

Shakespeare, William (1564-1616). Hamlet, act 2, sc.2, l. 249-50.

Thoreau, Henry David. Walden: An Annotated Edition. Edited by Walter Harding. New York: Houghton Mifflin, 1995.

Wade, Carole and Carol Tavris. Psychology, Sixth Edition. Upper Saddle River, New Jersey: Prentice-Hall, Inc, 2000.

Book Beneficiaries

In addition to the individual charities, causes and organizations identified by individual authors in their biographies, partial proceeds from all book sales of *Lessons from the Road: Inspirational Insights by Leading Speakers in Education* will be donated directly by the publisher to the following two non-profit organizations dedicated to the service of humanity:

ACPA Foundation. Founded in 1994, the ACPA Foundation seeks philanthropic support for the research, scholarship, professional development and leadership programs of ACPA—an organization dedicated to the enhancement of the student affairs profession and generation and dissemination of knowledge about students in higher education. More specifically, the Foundation's goal is to provide opportunities for college student educators to enhance their talents, experiences and skills enabling them to better prepare students for future leadership roles in a global society. For additional information go to: www.acpafoundation.org.

Alternatives in Motion. Alternatives in Motion firmly believes everyone should have the opportunity to participate in society and not be hindered by mobility issues. Founded in 1995, Alternatives in Motion provides new made-to-order wheelchairs and other mobility devices to people who need them but cannot afford them, and who don't qualify for any other financial assistance. They strive to help individuals improve and maintain their dignity and quality of life through mobility assistance. For additional information go to: www.alternativesinmotion.org.

Book Ordering Information

For additional copies of *Lessons from the Road: Inspirational Insights by Leading Speakers in Education*, or to inquire about how to order discounted quantities for your association meetings, leadership conferences, classes, professional staff development, bookstores and so on, contact the publisher directly at:

Zing! Leadership Development Systems, LLC
Box 1041
Marion, MA 02738
1.888.566.7536
VISIT: www.zingleadership.com

Leadership
Development Systems, LLC

Just add people.

It's ZING! Time...

Zing! Leadership Development Systems, LLC is dedicated to providing leadership development resources for those reaching and teaching leadership to high school students, college students and professional educators. Divided into three divisions, ZLDS, LLC offers innovative leadership development curriculum, conference resources and products, and ocean side personalized retreats—just add people! Quite simply, our mission is to provide you with all the tools you need to inspire those you serve around the original theme of ZING!. To discover more about the power and popularity of ZING!, go to www.zingleadership.com or call 1.888.566.7536.